COMPUTER COMPANION SERIES

The Sage Companion

PETER GOSLING

Paradigm

Paradigm Publishing Ltd.
131 Holland Park Avenue,
London W11 4UT

First edition 1988

© Peter Gosling 1988

British Library Cataloguing in Publication Data

Gosling, P. E. (Peter Edward).
   The Sage companion.
   1. Accounting. Applications of microcomputer
systems. Software packages. Sage
   I. Title
   657′.028′55369

ISBN 0-94882-566-9

Typeset by Mathematical Composition Setters Ltd, Salisbury and Printed in
Great Britain by Hollen Street Press Ltd, Slough, Berks.

About the Series

This series of books fills the need for a source of easy-to-understand guides to the many software packages and computer systems available. Titles will cover microcomputers, operating systems, computer applications, specialised software packages and communications.

Written in a simple and readable style, the books aim to provide a practical working knowledge of the most widely used computing packages to help serious computer users — both in business and at home — make better use of their machines. While these books do not attempt to tell the reader everything about a specific package, they provide an easy familiarisation guide which bridges the gap between the manual and a costly training course.

The authors are experts in their field and proven writers, which ensures accuracy of material and a uniformly high quality of content.

The series presents the information using non-technical language with clear, concise text and contains a variety of carefully structured examples for hands-on experience. The books will be equally useful for the experienced user looking for new applications and for those people looking for new software packages or equipment.

About this Companion

Now that powerful microcomputers are finding their way into smaller and smaller businesses one of the most useful and cost-effective programs is the accounting program. There are a number of these available and one of the most popular is the SAGE system. This is available in four 'flavours'. For the smallest business there is the SAGE BOOKKEEPER which will handle accounts in the simplest way. It consists of a Sales Ledger, Purchase Ledger and Nominal Ledger. Your VAT returns can be compiled with this program and a trial balance and audit trail are available. This will cope with up to 1000 customers and 1000 suppliers.

The BOOKKEEPER can be upgraded to the SAGE ACCOUNTANT for a slightly larger business with up to 5000 customers and 5000 suppliers. In addition this package includes a Report Generator and will allow you to send debt chasing letters and statements.

The next stage up is the SAGE ACCOUNTANT PLUS which combines the features of the BOOKKEEPER and ACCOUNTANT together with invoicing and stock control. The SAGE FINANCIAL CONTROLLER is the most comprehensive package in the range and includes all the features of the three systems mentioned plus Sales and Purchase Order Processing. In addition it will allow you to operate a parent company's accounts together with those of a number of subsidiary companies. A multi-user version of SAGE FINANCIAL CONTROLLER is also available.

This Companion is divided into five sections. The first tells you how to set up your SAGE system. The next three take you through the features of the different packages: Section 2 describes the features common to all four packages; Section 3 covers the features common to ACCOUNTANT, ACCOUNTANT PLUS and FINANCIAL CONTROLLER; similarly, Section 4 covers common areas of the ACCOUNTANT PLUS and FINANCIAL CONTROLLER. The final section relates to the additional features of FINANCIAL CONTROLLER.

The aim of the Sage Companion is to present to the non-accountant a simple and logical method of keeping accounts. There is also no need for the reader to be a computer expert to use any of the SAGE packages. The essential steps in setting up your SAGE system are described in the first section of the Companion as are the operations necessary in ensuring the safety and integrity of your records.

Contents

Acknowledgements

The author wishes to thank Bob Freeman and SAGESOFT Plc, particularly Graham Wylie, for help in the production of this Companion.

Note: As this Companion was being compiled there was a change in the VAT laws due to come into effect in October 1987. It applies to companies whose annual turnover is less than £250 000. Such companies need not pay their VAT on sales until they have received payment. Existing SAGE users will be informed of the procedure necessary to update their programs in the SAGE Technical Bulletin, **SageTech**.

There are a number of Sage Factsheets available that answer some of the common queries made about SAGE accounting programs. These are available from Sagesoft.

1 Introduction

Setting up your system; the PASSWORD program;
the INSTALL program; using twin floppy and hard
disk systems; backing up your files; Passwords, setting
up your printer

When you receive your copy of the SAGE program you will
have to make a copy of it before you do anything else. This
means that your working disk will be a copy of the original
disk. SAGE always prints the company name at the top of
every report. This information, which includes the company's
full name and address must be entered and recorded on the
working disk the first time it is used.

Once you have made your copy put the master disk in a
safe place and use the copy for your everyday work. If you
have a computer with a hard disk then you can copy the
program, making sure that you have set up a special directory
to receive it.

On starting up your new SAGE system — on the copy of
the master disk, of course — the screen will display Fig. 1.1.
You will then enter the name of your company followed by

```
S A G E S O F T   A C C O U N T A N T   P L U S - V2.2
         Copyright  (C)  Sagesoft PLC 1985, 1986
              Telephone  (091) 284 7077

     Please enter your name and address below:

        Enter Name ?
```

Fig. 1.1.

four address lines. This will personalize your copy of the program so that whenever you run it the first display will be of your company name and address. This also provides the heading to be printed on every report and statement.

The INSTALL program allows you to customize SAGE to your requirements. As the SAGE systems are delivered they are already configured for you to run on a twin floppy disk system. If you want to change to a hard disk or a single floppy disk system then INSTALL will need to be run. Any user who has either the SAGE ACCOUNTANT PLUS or SAGE FINANCIAL CONTROLLER is advised to run on a hard disk machine or you will find that there is a severe restriction in the size of ledgers you can use. INSTALL is entered by the command

A > install

followed by the display shown in Fig. 1.2.
Reply to this with the appropriate drive letter. If you are using a computer such as the Amstrad[1] PC 1512 DD with two floppy disk drives, the system disk, that is the copy of the disk supplied by Sagesoft PLC, will go in drive A — the left hand drive. The disk that will contain the ledgers must be placed in the right hand drive, drive B; but more of that later.

If you are using a computer with a hard, winchester, disk drive and a single floppy disk drive such as the Amstrad PC 1512 HD, the program will be on drive C. The SAGE

```
**************************************************************
**  Sagesoft PLC            Install           Version 2.1  **
**                                                          **
**                                                          **
**  This Installation program must be used in conjunction  **
**  with SAGE 16Bit Account Software Only.  The routine    **
**  will allow you to change the following :               **
**                                                          **
**       Screen, Keyboard, Printer, Disk Drives            **
**                                                          **
**                                                          **
**                                                          **
**************************************************************

         On which Drive is 'SAGE.INS' (A - P) ?
```

Fig. 1.2.

[1] Amstrad is a trademark of Amstrad Consumer Electronics Plc

programs supplied by Sagesoft PLC should be copied into a
directory on the hard disk: you should have already created a
special directory for these programs on the hard disk by the
command

C > md sage

Copy the files from the floppy disk in drive A, the single disk
drive, into that directory. The ledger files will be created on
your hard disk.

You can use SAGE on a computer with a single floppy disk
drive only, such as the Amstrad PC 1512 SD. As the SAGE
programs reside in memory while they are running the single
drive can be used for the ledgers.

When using a hard disk system you must enter the directory
using the command

C > cd \sage

and then copy all the SAGE programs from the disk or disks
supplied into this directory. Place the floppy disk into the
floppy disk drive and use the DOS **copy** command

C > copy a:*.*

You will then need to run INSTALL in order to tell SAGE
that you are now running on a hard disk system.

The Install program will allow you to make modifications to
your system by defining the drives on which certain ledgers
and documents are stored. It also allows you to define the
codes needed to print condensed or expanded characters on
your printer when you are printing reports and statements. As
delivered, SAGE will be set up to use the most common codes
but these can be altered if your printer is not one of the most
common types. After you have stated the drive containing the
programs, which will usually be A for a floppy disk machine
and C for a hard disk machine, you are shown a further
selection of options (Fig. 1.3).
It is unlikely that you will have to modify the first three, but
the fourth, Option D, if chosen will result in the display
shown in Fig. 1.4.

The first two options as set up show that the data, i.e. the

```
SAGE SOFTWARE INSTALLATION ROUTINE

A).   Screen Controls
B).   Keyboard Controls
C).   Printer Controls
D).   Accounts Program Control
E).   Keyboard Test

X).   Exit from program

Which Option?
```

Fig. 1.3.

ledgers, are on the disk in drive B, the stock details are on drive A, the existing drive for the program is A and the report generators are on drive B.

The function key for the standard VAT rate is defined by the two codes 84 and 49 as key F3. The last option, which will almost certainly have to be reset, defines the number of decimal places on invoices in the quantity field and the unit price field. As shown in the illustration the unit price will be in pence, hence two decimal places, and the quantity in whole numbers, hence the zero number of decimal places. The invoice lead option, if set on by placing a 1 in the third column, creates invoice numbers with leading zeros.

If you are using SAGE on a hard disk machine then you must tell the program that you are going to locate all the files on drive C. This means that you will have to make sure that the options are displayed as shown in Fig. 1.5.

At regular intervals, probably once a day, you will need to take security copies of your SAGE ledgers. If you are using a twin floppy disk system then once you have left SAGE you can copy them using the DOS **copy** command. If you are using a hard disk then it is better to archive your ledgers onto floppy disks using the **backup** and **restore** routines. Their use

```
ACCOUNTS PROGRAM CONTROL

A).  Data Drive   / Stock  Drive  [A=0] [B=1]    1    0    0    0    0
B).  Exist Drive  / Repgen Drive  [A=0] [B=1]    0    1    0    0    0
C).  Hard Disk Option     [Off = 0] [On = 1]     0    0    0    0    0
D).  One Disk Option      [Off = 0] [On = 1]     0    0    0    0    0
E).  Taxkey  e..g.  T1                          84   49    0    0    0
F).  Qty D.P. / Unit D.P. / Invoice lead [ ][0]  0    2    0    0    0

X).  Return to Menu

Which Line?
```

Fig. 1.4

```
ACCOUNTS PROGRAM CONTROL

A).   Data Drive    / Stock   Drive  [A=0] [B=1]    2    2    0    0    0
B).   Exist Drive   / Repgen  Drive  [A=0] [B=1]    2    2    0    0    0
C).   Hard Disk Option       [Off = 0] [On = 1]     1    0    0    0    0
D).   One Disk Option        [Off = 0] [On = 1]     0    0    0    0    0
E).   Taxkey    e..g.  T1                          84   49    0    0    0
F).   Qty D.P. / Unit D.P. / Invoice lead [ ][0]    0    2    0    0    0

X).   Return to Menu

Which Line?
```

Fig. 1.5

is fully described in the installation notes supplied with your system.

Before running the SAGE system you will have to set up your own password in order to ensure that no unauthorized person can have access to your accounts. As supplied, SAGE provides you with a ready-made password — 'LETMEIN'. The PASSWORD program on the program disk allows you to change that if you wish.

In order to do this type the command

PASSWORD

and the display shown in Fig. 1.6 appears on the screen. In order to see what the current password is, together with the parts of the package protected by it, all that is needed is for you to type

A > password v

and the system will allow you to view all the available

```
A>password

Usage : PASSWORD <option> <password> <menus>

<option>    :- XAU  - To Append a password
               XDU  - To Delete a password
               XVU  - To View a password

<password> :- Actual Password Text

<menus>    :- SP  - Sales Ledger Postings    ST  - Stock Control
              SR  - Sales Ledger Reports     SO  - Sales Order Proc.
              PP  - Purchase Ledger Postings PO  - Purchase Order
              PR  - Purchase Ledger Reports  IV  - Invoicing
              NP  - Nominal Ledger Postings  PY  - Payroll
              NR  - Nominal Ledger Reports   ALL - All Menus
              MR  - Management Reports
```

Fig. 1.6

passwords and the ledgers they refer to. It will respond with

LETMEIN : SP SR PP PR NP NR MR ST SO PO IV PY

To append a new password you need to enter the appropriate command together with the new password followed by the sections to be protected by it. **ALL** will protect all the sections.

A > password a snoopy all

and

A > password d letmein all

will delete the named password. The first word you type in is the name of the program you are using ('PASSWORD' is the program you intend to run, the 'a' or 'd' indicate that you are appending or deleting a password. The next set of characters tell the program which password you are either appending to the system or deleting from it. Finally the word 'all' indicates that the password refers to access to all the ledgers in the system).

All SAGE systems are delivered configured in such a way as to work with the most popular types of printers. If you find that yours does not work for some reason then you will have to run INSTALL and examine the printer codes. INSTALL allows you to change these, but unless you are familiar with this aspect of using computers you should consult your SAGE dealer together with the printer manual to ensure that you are making the printer work properly for you.

It is probably better to use SAGE in conjunction with a dot matrix printer rather than the daisy wheel type as most of the SAGE output is printed in condensed print and when printing invoices it prints the form along with the invoice; a feature which might be difficult for some daisy wheel printers to do.

2 Sage Bookkeeper, Sage Accountant, Sage Accountant plus and Sage Financial Controller

2.1. Introduction; 2.2. The nominal ledger, entering the accounts; 2.3. The sales and purchase ledgers, entering the accounts; 2.4. The sales, purchase and nominal ledgers, posting to accounts; 2.5. Nominal ledger reports; 2.6. Sales and purchase ledger reports; 2.7. Management reports, VAT analysis, audit trail, trial balance; 2.8. End of month and end of year procedures

2.1 Introduction

The structure of the SAGE accounting system programs is shown in Fig. 2.1.1. Always enter the system via the main menu: all of them, BOOKKEEPER, ACCOUNTANT, ACCOUNTANT PLUS and FINANCIAL CONTROLLER have the same structure. The Sales and Purchase Ledgers contain details of your transactions with customers and suppliers and these are both linked to the Nominal Ledger via Nominal Codes. These are codes that are allocated to transactions in order to identify their type. For example, you may have a code, say 1000, that is allocated to training. It may be that your company supplies training and at the same

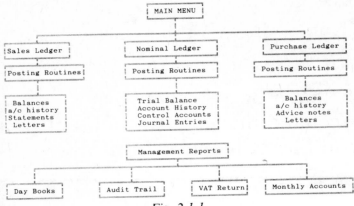

Fig. 2.1.1.

time may have to buy in certain types of training. It follows that an entry into the Sales Ledger for the sale of a training course is identified by the nominal code 1000. In addition, if you buy in some training then this too is identified by the nominal code 1000. These two entries are made in the Nominal Ledger and from this one can compare the income from and the expenditure on training. This is a very simple example of a Nominal Ledger report.

Reporting is an integral part of the SAGE system since by inspection of the ledgers you can quickly find the outstanding amounts owed to you by any or all of your customers and, similarly, you can find out exactly the extent of your current debts.

The management reports are obtained from the three ledgers and will provide essential information for you, particularly the VAT return and the monthly accounts.

Invoicing is carried out as a separate function; when creating an invoice you can do so either without any reference to stock and customers, or by using references to the Sales Ledger and Stock files to save typing details of names, addresses, prices and quantities. After an invoice has been created you can update the ledgers if you wish. Obviously, if you are running a totally integrated system you will want to post the details to the appropriate accounts, but it is not necessary if you have a reason for not requiring it.

Additional to the ledger functions and the management reports each system offers a set of 'utilities'. The utilities allow you to insert changes in the tax codes, reconfigure your ledgers when space has become tight, i.e. if they are full of accounts which are inactive or show a zero balance, and handle the processes that need to be carried at month-end and year-end.

In order of sophistication the four related SAGE programs described in this Companion are BOOKKEEPER, ACCOUNTANT, ACCOUNTANT PLUS and FINANCIAL CONTROLLER. The difference between them lies in the facilities offered. The system appropriate to your business can be decided upon from the following information.

Bookkeeper

This offers the three main ledgers but without reporting facilities such as the production of a balance sheet. It does, however, provide a report in the form of a 'quick ratio' allowing you to discover the comparison between the amounts outstanding on two or more accounts. The BOOKKEEPER is suitable for the small business where the number of Sales, Purchase and Nominal accounts do not exceed 1000.

BOOKKEEPER will produce a Profit and Loss account, Aged Debtor's information, Trial Balance, VAT Return and Audit Trail. In addition it will handle special VAT schemes for Retailers. This system would in fact work quite satisfactorily on a single disk drive computer.

Accountant

This will offer everything that BOOKKEEPER does but for upwards of 5000 Sales and Purchase accounts and 1000 Nominal accounts. Additional reporting functions are available so that debt chasing letters can be generated, statements and remittance advice notes can be printed, a Sales/Purchase analysis produced and an analysis made of sales and purchases by department. Both a balance sheet and a profit and loss account can be produced from this system.

Accountant Plus

The third member of the family possesses all the features of the other two plus the ability to create invoices and carry out a stock control function. Additional reporting facilities are provided as well as price list generation, credit note production and stock valuation.

Financial Controller

This system offers the most features. As well as all the facilities provided by the other three systems it can be used by more than one user at a time and can concurrently handle the accounts for more than one company. Sales Order and Purchase Order processing are fully integrated with their appropriate ledgers.

The main menu for Accountant Plus is shown in Fig. 2.1.2. For all systems except BOOKKEEPER you can if you wish decide on and enter the details of the various departments that are going to be your cost centres. These departments are referred to during the entry of all the transactions and can then be used for the various analyses that can be performed at the end of the year. Choose the **Departments** option from the **Utilities** option on the main menu. The whole menu displayed is

> Initialisation
> Departments
> Reconfiguration
> Tax Code Changes
> DOS Functions
> Text Editor
>
> Main Menu

On choosing **Departments** you are given the option to **View** or **Edit**. You must first of all create the department numbers using the Edit option; you do this my moving the highlight to

```
┌──────────────────────────────────────────────────────────────────────┐
│ Main Menu              Accountant Plus              Date : 270187      │
└──────────────────────────────────────────────────────────────────────┘

                         No. of entries : 0

┌──────────────────────────────────────────────────────────────────────┐
│  Sales Ledger Postings              Stock Control                      │
│  Sales Ledger Reports               Invoice Production                 │
│                                                                        │
│  Purchase Ledger Postings           Management Reports                 │
│  Purchase Ledger Reports            Utilities Routines                 │
│                                                                        │
│  Nominal Ledger Postings            Quit                               │
│  Nominal Ledger Reports                                                │
└──────────────────────────────────────────────────────────────────────┘
```

Fig. 2.1.2.

Edit with the right arrow key, →, and typing the department
numbers each followed by their description. For example,
Department 1 might be **Shop No. 1**, Department 2 might be
Shop No. 2 and Department 3 **Shop No. 3** and so on.
Choosing the **View** option will allow you to display the list of
departments on the screen or the printer.

2.2   The Nominal Ledger, entering the accounts

Once you have your system running you must set up the
various accounts together with their identifiers and names.
The first one to do is the Nominal Ledger and in the first
instance you must select the **Utilities Routines** option again
from the main menu.

Choose the **Initialisation** option from the sub menu and you
are presented with the screen in Fig. 2.2.1

The suppliers of SAGE recommend that you use the
following codes for the accounts listed above. These are

0038 — Debtor's Control
0065 — Creditor's Control
0089 — Bank Account
0088 — Cash Account
0069 — Tax Account
1099 — Discount Account

When you have entered these Nominal Account codes they

```
Initialisation              Accountant Plus           Date : 270187
```

```
                    This will clean the data files
                    Existing data will be destroyed


        Number of Sales    Accounts:
        Number of Purchase Accounts:
        Number of Nominal  Accounts:


        Debtor's Control    N/C Number:
        Creditor's Control N/C Number:
        Bank N/C Number            :
        Cash N/C Number            :
        Tax Control N/C Number     :
        Discount N/C Number        :

            Press ESC on the discount entry to continue
```

Fig. 2.2.1.

will be created on the data disk; this takes a little time and
after they have been created you will be asked if you have any
data files already. As you are just starting off answer **NO** to
the question, as you have no data files yet. Press the **ESC** key
to return to the main menu.

On your return to the main menu you need to allocate the
other Nominal Account codes. These are all four digit
numbers and a suggested method of numbering is given in
your manual:

0000	– 0009	Fixed assets
0035	– 0089	Current assets and liabilities
0090	– 0099	Financed by
1000	– 1099	Trading accounts (Sales)
2000	– 2099	Trading accounts (Purchases)
2500	– 2510	Trading accounts (Expenses)
3000	– 3500	Profit and Loss account

From the main menu select **Nominal Ledger Postings** and
from its sub menu choose **Nominal Accounts**. The screen will
now look like Fig. 2.2.2.

```
Nominal Accounts            Accountant Plus           Date : 270187
```

```
    Account Reference :
```

Fig. 2.2.2.

Enter the account code and you will be asked

Is this a new account: No Yes

You will answer by pressing **Y** or moving the highlight to be over the word **Yes**. Press Return.

If you decide that Nominal Code 2510 will relate to labour charges with an annual budget of £2400 then the entry will be as shown in Fig. 2.2.3.

You are not forced to enter an amount for the yearly budget. If you do enter it then SAGE will allocate the monthly amounts automatically. Alternatively you can enter the individual monthly budgets. Press **ESC** when you have finished and you are asked for another Nominal Code. When you have finished entering the Nominal Codes, press **ESC** again and you are returned to the main menu.

When you have entered all your Nominal Codes you will need to have a printed copy of these for your records. They can, of course, be added to or modified at any time.

Having returned to the main menu, by pressing the **Esc** key, move the highlight to **Nominal Ledger Reports** and press the Return key. Select **Account Names** from the new menu displayed; first you will be asked for the range of account numbers to be listed. If you press the Return key for each of these SAGE will automatically select the range to be from the highest to the lowest and thus include every account code allocated. You have a choice of displaying the accounts on the screen or printing them out. It is probably a good idea to have them displayed first to see if you have included all you

```
 Nominal Accounts              Accountant Plus              Date : 270187

        Account Reference : 2510

        Account Name      : Labour Charges

        Yearly Budget     : 2400

     Month 1  :   200.00          Month  7  :   200.00
     Month 2  :   200.00          Month  8  :   200.00
     Month 3  :   200.00          Month  9  :   200.00
     Month 4  :   200.00          Month 10  :   200.00
     Month 5  :   200.00          Month 11  :   200.00
     Month 6  :   200.00          Month 12  :   200.00
```

Fig. 2.2.3.

PETER GOSLING

Nominal Ledger Reports - Account Names.

Ref.	Account Name	Ref.	Account Name	Ref.	Account Name
0100	Sierra	0101	Sierra depreciation	0120	Metro
0121	Metro depreciation	0130	Lada Estate	0131	Lada depreciation
0140	Fixtures and Fittings	0200	Bank	0210	Cash
0220	Debtor's Control	0320	Tax Control	0330	Creditors Control
0400	Directors Loan Account	0410	Share Capital	0420	Retained Profit
1010	Hard Disk PC Sales	1020	Twin Disk PC Sales	1030	Single Disk PC Sales
1110	Dot Matrix Printer Sales	1120	NLQ Printer Sales	1130	Daisy Wheel Printer Sales
1210	Accounting S'ware Sales	1220	Comms Software Sales	1230	Bus. Risk S'ware Sales
1240	Data Base S'ware Sales	1250	W.Proc. S'ware Sales	1310	Listing Paper Sales
1320	Invoice Stationery Sales	1321	Statement Sales	1323	Other Document Sales
1330	Accessory Sales	1340	Floppy Disk Sales	1341	Micro Floppy Sales
2010	Hard Disk PC Purchases	2020	Twin Disk PC Purchases	2030	Single Disk PC Purchases
2110	D Matrix Printer Purch.	2120	NLQ Printer Purch.	2130	Daisy Wheel Printer Purch
2210	Accounting S'ware Purch	2220	Comms. S'ware Purchases	2230	Bus. Risk S'ware Purch
2240	Data Base S'ware Purch	2250	W.Proc. S'ware Purchases	2310	Listing Paper Purchases
2320	Invoice Stat. Purchases	2330	Accessory Purchases	2340	Floppy Disk Purchases
2341	Micro Floppy Sales	3010	Hotel Accommodation	3020	Entertainment
3030	Sundry Expenses	3040	General Office Overheads	3050	
3100	Petrol	3150	Motor Expenses	3210	Rent and Rates
3220	Gas and Electricity	3230	Telephone Charges	3300	Directors Salaries
3310	Staff Salaries	3320	Casual Labour	3400	Postage
3410	Carriers	3500	Equipment Rental	3510	Building Repairs/Renewals
3520	Stationery	3600	Advertising	3620	Sundries
3999	Discount				

Fig. 2.2.4.

need. Having done that call up the option again but select a printed output this time. The printed output would look as shown in Fig. 2.2.4.

As you will almost certainly have some amounts already allocated to some of the accounts from your previous accounting system you will need to post some opening balances to the various accounts. Choose the **Nominal Ledger Reports** from the main menu and from the next menu choose **Nominal Ledger Postings**. This displays the screen shown in Fig. 2.2.5.

From this sub menu choose the **Journal Entries** option. Enter the opening balances via the next screen, Fig. 2.2.6.

For the opening balances the Reference must be entered as **O/BAL**, the details must be entered as **Opening Balance** and under **Tc** the tax code must be entered as **T9**. (The details of VAT codes will be dealt with later.) Take note of the instruction that the batch total, which is the sum of the debits and credits, must be zero when you leave this screen. To leave this screen press the **Esc** key. If the batch total is not zero then you will not be allowed to leave the screen; you will have to edit the entries until this situation is reached. The department code, details and the Nominal Account code must all have been prepared by you before entering these opening balances. Check the batch total manually — enter onto the screen in batches of ten entries before you start, in order to avoid this problem. Once you have returned to the Main Menu you

```
┌─────────────────────────────────────────────────────────────┐
│  Nominal Ledger Postings    Accountant Plus                  │
│                                               Date : 270187   │
└─────────────────────────────────────────────────────────────┘
```

```
        ┌───────────────────────────────────┐
        │                                   │
        │     Nominal Accounts              │
        │     Bank Payments                 │
        │     Bank Receipts                 │
        │     Cash Payments                 │
        │     Cash Receipts                 │
        │     Journal Entries               │
        │                                   │
        │                                   │
        │     Main Menu                     │
        │                                   │
        └───────────────────────────────────┘
```

Fig. 2.2.5.

```
┌─────────────────────────────────────────────────────────────────────┐
│ Journal Entries          Accountant Plus           Date : 270187     │
└─────────────────────────────────────────────────────────────────────┘
```

```
        Date :                           Reference  :
  N/C Name  :                            Batch Total:    00.00


          N/C    Dep.      Details      Tc      Debit     Credit
```

Batch Total <u>MUST</u> be <u>ZERO</u> before exit

Fig. 2.2.6.

should choose the Nominal Ledger Reports option. From this you will be able to list on the screen or, preferably, on your printer all the nominal codes in order and the accounts they refer to. You then have a permanent copy of these codes.

2.3   The Sales and Purchase Ledgers, entering the accounts

The next task is to enter the Sales Ledger accounts. This is done in a similar way to the entry of the nominal codes. Choose Sales Ledger Postings from the Main Menu and from the next menu presented to you choose the Sales Accounts option. The screen will be as shown in Fig. 2.3.1.

Each account is identified by a unique code that can contain up to six alphabetic and numeric characters. You can devise a simple set of codes incorporating the name of the account thus making it easier to locate when it comes to posting to that account. For example if you were setting up an account for a company called JASON INDUSTRIES then the account reference could be JASON. When the account reference is first entered the system will have no knowledge of it and so will ask the question **Is this a new account? No Yes**. As it is a new account you answer in the affirmative by either typing **Y** or moving the highlight over the **Yes** by means of the right arrow key. In the part of the box beside **Account Name** the

```
┌─────────────────────────────────────────────────────────────────┐
│ Sales Accounts          Accountant Plus            Date : 270187  │
└─────────────────────────────────────────────────────────────────┘
        Account Reference   :   ┌─────────────┐
                                └─────────────┘

            Account Name    :   ┌─────────────────────────────┐
                Address     :   │                             │
                  "         :   │                             │
                  "         :   │                             │
                  "         :   │                             │
                                │                             │
           Credit Limit     :   │                             │
               Turnover     :   │                             │
                                │                             │
           Telephone No.    :   │                             │
           Contact Name     :   │                             │
              Sort Code     :   │                             │
        VAT Registration    :   └─────────────────────────────┘
```

Fig. 2.3.1.

words **UNUSED ACCOUNT NAME** will appear. As soon as
you enter the name of the company this message will vanish
to be replaced by the account name. The rest of the screen is
filled just as a form is filled in. The result will look as shown
in Fig. 2.3.2.

It is not necessary to enter a sort code or the VAT registration
number unless they are going to be used for generating reports
using the Report Generator. On finishing the entries press **Esc**
for the next blank screen to be filled in. Continue this until all
the account details have been entered. Press **Esc** again to
return to the Main Menu. In order to list the accounts select
Sales Ledger Reports from the Main Menu and choose
Account Names from the next menu. Then you can obtain a

```
┌─────────────────────────────────────────────────────────────────┐
│ Sales Accounts          Accountant Plus            Date : 270187  │
└─────────────────────────────────────────────────────────────────┘
        Account Reference   :   ┌─────────────┐
                                │ JASON       │
                                └─────────────┘
            Account Name    :   ┌─────────────────────────────┐
                Address     :   │ Jason Industries Ltd        │
                  "         :   │ Unit 12, Beech Industrial Est│
                  "         :   │ Freshwater                  │
                  "         :   │ Somerset                    │
                                │ WL3 5TF                     │
           Credit Limit     :   │ 1500                        │
               Turnover     :   │                             │
                                │                             │
           Telephone No.    :   │  0345-56789                 │
           Contact Name     :   │  W.Smithers                 │
              Sort Code     :   │                             │
        VAT Registration    :   └─────────────────────────────┘
```

Fig. 2.3.2.

PETER GOSLING   Sales Ledger Reports - Account Names.   Date : 010386
Page : 1

Ref.	Account Name	Ref.	Account Name	Ref.	Account Name
AXGRO	Axgro Foods Ltd.	BELL	Bell Brothers Ltd	BROWN	Brown Bros. Ltd.
CBL	C.B.Ltd.	DUN	Dun Distributors,	FORD	Ford Fish Factory,
GRBEN	Greens Greengrocery,	JASON	Jason Industries Ltd	LONG	Longlife Roof Felters,
MILD	Mild Steel Fabrications,	MILES	Miles of Yarn Ltd.	MILLS	Mills Milliners,
ORANGE	Orange Electrics,	RED	Red Books Ltd.,	TEST	Test Services Ltd
ZZPOP	ZZPOP Ltd.				

PETER GOSLING   Purchase Ledger Reports - Account Names.   Date : 010386
Page : 1

Ref.	Account Name	Ref.	Account Name	Ref.	Account Name
ABLE	Able Electronics Ltd.	BAKER	Baker & Co.	CHARLI	Charlies Paper Mill.
DELTA	Delta Design Ltd	ECHO	Echo Electronics Ltd.	FOX	Fox Micro Components,
SAGE	SAGESOFT PLC	TEST	TEST Supplier ltd		

Fig. 2.3.3.

list either on the screen or on your printer just as you did with the Nominal Accounts.

The same procedure applies exactly for the creation of the Purchase Ledger Accounts. As the two ledgers are quite separate you can use the same code names in each ledger should you wish to do so; this will not confuse SAGE at all.

A typical printout of account names from the Sales and Purchase Ledgers is shown in Fig. 2.3.3.

2.4   The Sales, Purchase and Nominal Ledgers, Posting to accounts

Once the ledgers and the accounts they contain have been set up you can begin posting invoices and receipts to them. The screens displayed used for posting to all these three accounts are very similar. If you choose Sales Ledger Postings from the Main Menu you will get a sub menu of four choices:

> Sales Accounts
> Sales Invoices
> Sales Credit Notes
> Sales Receipts
>
> Main Menu

The choices are selected by pressing the up or down arrow keys and although you can return to the Main Menu in this way you can save time simply by pressing the **Esc** key.

The first choice has already been dealt with; it allows you to add new accounts to the ledger. Selection of the second choice provides you with the ability to post invoices to selected accounts. You are presented with the screen shown in Fig. 2.4.1.

The entries to the ledgers are made by filling in the screen column by column. The **A/C** entry is the account code, as set up previously. After you have entered the code SAGE searches for the account name and displays it in the **A/C Name** box. If the code cannot be found you will not be allowed to proceed. Only when a valid account code has been entered will you be able to go on to the next column. The date must always be

```
┌─────────────────────────────────────────────────────────────────────┐
│  Sales Invoices            Accountant Plus              Date : 270187 │
└─────────────────────────────────────────────────────────────────────┘

A/C Name :                                      Tax Rate    :
N/C Name :                                      Batch Total :     0.00

A/C    Date    Inv.    N/C    Dep.      Details    Nett Amnt  Tc Tax Amnt
  ┌───────────────────────────────────────────────────────────────────┐
  │                                                                     │
  │                                                                     │
  │                                                                     │
  │                                                                     │
  │                                                                     │
  │                                                                     │
  └───────────────────────────────────────────────────────────────────┘

                                                    0.00       0.00
```

Fig. 2.4.1.

entered as a six digit number, so that 9 February 1988 would
be entered as 090288. Sage checks that this is a valid date
before proceeding. You must check that the year is correct,
particularly in the early months of a new year. Once the
posting has been made you may have difficulty in
correcting the mistake. The **N/C** column will have the
Nominal Code to which the entry is to be allocated and once
a valid code has been entered the appropriate account name is
displayed in the **N/C Name** box at the top of the screen. **Dep**.
refers to the cost centre to which the invoice is to be
allocated; you will have been able to set up a series of
departments, should you wish to do so, using the Utilities
option from the Main Menu. This operation is not essential
and SAGE takes no account of it in its general reporting.
However, you can make use of it if you wish to tailor your
own reports if your system has the Report Generator. Pressing
the **Return** key at this stage will result in a zero being placed
in the column. The **Details** entry will contain a brief
description of the contents of the invoice. The cash value of
the invoice is taken care of in the last three columns of the
entry. The **Nett Amount** entry can either be the actual net
amount of the invoice or the gross amount including VAT.
This is because SAGE can compute the correct entries
whatever the amount entered. The **Tc** entry is the VAT code
and in general, until the VAT laws change, this will be one of

the codes T0, T1, T2 or T9. The VAT rates currently associated with these codes are:

T0   –   Zero-rated
T1   –   Items rated at 15%
T2   –   VAT exempt items
T9   –   Non-VATable items

Enter the appropriate tax code and the amount of VAT is automatically calculated and entered into the **Tax Amnt** box. If you enter the gross amount into the **Net Amnt** box you can save yourself the trouble of calculating the net amount and the tax by pressing the < key after you have entered the tax code. Two examples will demonstrate this.

1   If you enter 50 in the **Nett Amnt** box and T1 in the **Tc** box you will automatically get 7.50 displayed in the **Tax Amnt** box.
2   If you enter 57.50, the gross amount, in the **Nett Amnt** box and T1 in the **Tc** box you will first get 8.63 displayed under **Tax Amnt**. This is obviously incorrect. To correct it press the < key and you will find that the entries will adjust themselves to the same values as in the first example.

Notice how the **Tax Rate** and **Batch Total** boxes reflect the tax rate of the current entry and the total so far entered. The two totals under the **Nett Amnt** and **Tax Amnt** columns are automatically totalled. This enables you to check your entries against your written information. No posting has yet been done so you can edit the information while it is displayed on the screen.

General hints

Function keys:

F1   Enters the current date
F2   Repeats the entry directly above the cursor position
F3   Enters Tax Code T1

You can move around the screen in order to edit any entry by moving the arrow keys to take you to the entry you wish to change. You can do this at any time.

A typical screen is shown in Fig. 2.4.2. When the entries are complete press the Esc key and the prompt

Post Edit Abandon

is displayed at the bottom of the screen. If you are happy with the figures you have entered press the Return key to post to the ledger. Select **Edit** if you wish to change any of the entries; press **E** or move the cursor with the right arrow key and press Return. Select **Abandon** if you wish to ignore a whole screen of entries and return directly to the Main Menu; press **A** or use the right arrow key and press Return.

Once you have posted the entries you will be presented with a further blank screen. At this point you can make further entries or return to the Main Menu simply by pressing Esc again.

To enter a sales receipt choose the Sales Receipts option from the menu and you will see a display as shown in Fig. 2.4.3.

Enter the account reference to which the receipt is to be posted and SAGE will find and display the full company name in the top right hand corner. Next enter the date of banking the cheque, the cheque number and the full amount of the

Sales Invoices			Accountant Plus				Date :	270187	
A/C Name :Jason Industries Ltd						Tax Rate :		15.000	
N/C Name :Miscellaneous Purchases						Batch Total :		513.50	
A/C	Date	Inv.	N/C	Dep.	Details	Nett Amnt	Tc	Tax Amnt	
MMS	120387	00897	2001	0	Stationery	50.00	T1	7.50	
JASON	120387	00898	2005	0	Office Equpt	396.52	T1	59.48	

446.52   66.98

Fig. 2.4.2.

Sales Receipts		Accountant Plus				Date : 270187	

A/C Ref	:				A/C Name	:	
Payment Date	:						
Cheque No.	:						
Cheque Amount	:			Cheque Balance	:		

Payment	No.	Type	Date	Inv.	Details	Amount	Discount

Fig. 2.4.3.

cheque. A list of current unpaid invoices will then be displayed (*see* Fig. 2.4.4.).

If you have made an error in the initial entries — date, amount or account — you can exit by pressing the Esc key. This produces the prompt

Finish Continue Abandon

By choosing the **Automatic** option the payment is allocated to outstanding invoices from the top downwards. If you choose **Manual** you can scroll downwards through the list until you find the invoice against which the cheque is to be allocated. Should the invoice be further on in the ledger than the ten entries displayed then move the cursor to the bottom of the list and press Esc. This displays another ten invoices as yet unpaid. The Payment column will then be filled in with FULL

Sales Receipts		Accountant Plus				Date : 031087	

A/C Ref	: JASON				A/C Name	: Jason Industries Ltd	
Payment Date	: 031087						
Cheque No.	: 009521						
Cheque Amount	: 456.00			Cheque Balance	: 456.00		

Payment	No.	Type	Date	Inv.	Details	Amount	Discount
	62	SI	020987	00898	Office Equpt.	456.00	

Method of Payment : Automatic Manual

Fig. 2.4.4.

or PART according to whether the invoice is being paid in full or in part. If you have chosen the manual option and pressed the Return key when you have reached the invoice to be paid you will be asked

Type of Payment: Full Part Discount Cancel

This enables you to allocate payments correctly. The **Cancel** option allows you to correct a payment that has been allocated to the wrong invoice — so long as you have not posted it already!

Press the Esc key when you have completed the payments and the cheque balance, which is decremented each time a payment has been allocated, becomes zero. The prompt at the bottom then shows

Post Edit

By choosing **Edit** you can go back and change an allocation.

Credit notes are entered from the Credit Notes option and the entry is the same as the entry of invoice details. The screen display is as shown in Fig. 2.4.5. It is, however, possible to match a credit note against an invoice through the Sales Receipts routine by treating each credit note as a manual payment with a nil cheque value. This is done by paying off the credit note that has already been entered onto the ledger.

Sales Credit Notes				Accountant Plus			Date : 031087		
A/C Name :						Tax Rate :			
N/C Name :						Batch Total :			
A/C	Date	Inv.	N/C	Dep.	Details	Nett Amnt	Tc	Tax	Amnt
						0.00			0.00

Fig. 2.4.5.

This has the effect of increasing the cheque balance as shown at the top of the screen. That amount is then used to pay off the outstanding invoice amount.

Purchase Ledger invoice postings are done in exactly the same way and when the Purchase Ledger Postings option is chosen from the Main Menu a sub menu similar to the Sales Ledger Postings' sub menu is displayed

> Purchase Accounts
> Purchase Invoices
> Purchase Credit Notes
> Purchase Payments
>
> Main Menu

Select **Purchase Invoices** and a screen identical to the Sales Ledger invoices screen is displayed. It is completed in the same way as for Sales invoices.

The screen for the entry of Sales and Purchase Ledger Credit Notes also follows this same format and is handled in exactly the same way as for entering invoices.

Nominal Ledger entries are selected from a sub menu displayed when the **Nominal Ledger Postings** option is chosen from the Main Menu. Its list of choices is longer than for the other two ledgers and has the following choices:

> Nominal Accounts
> Bank Payments
> Bank Receipts
> Cash Payments
> Cash Receipts
> Journal Entries
>
> Main Menu

Again the **Nominal Accounts** option allows you to edit the Nominal Account names and add new accounts. The next four options produce screens almost identical with those used when posting invoices and credit notes to the other two ledgers except that this time the posting is to the Bank Account or the Cash Account.

Should you wish to delete an account from a ledger then

you may do so only if the account has a zero balance. To delete the account all you have to do is to go to the **Account Names** option on the Postings menu and replace the account name with the words **UNUSED ACCOUNT NAME**. This will not delete the account immediately but when you perform the end of the month reconfiguration routine, as described on page 52, or an Initialisation, the account will be removed from the ledger.

The screen used to make Journal Entries has already been shown on page 16.

2.5   Nominal Ledger Reports

On choosing the **Nominal Ledger Reports** option from the Main Menu you will be presented with a sub menu with six options; five options if you are using SAGE BOOKKEEPER.

> Account Names
> Trial Balance
> Quick Ratio
> Account History
> Control Accounts
> Report Generator
>
> Main Menu

The option not available on SAGE BOOKKEEPER is the Report Generator and its description is covered in Chapter 3, Section 3.1.

The Account Names option will produce a list of the Nominal Ledger codes and the account names, as described earlier. The Trial Balance option will produce an up-to-date listing of the Nominal Accounts in the form shown in Fig. 2.5.1 in debit or credit columns with sub-totals that must be equal. If they are not then there is some fault, probably in the hardware. Should there not be a balance between the total debit and credit accounts you should go back to the most recent back-up copy of the ledgers and produce a trial balance from there. You may then have to re-enter the latest data and try again.

The Quick Ratio report will give you the relationship

between sets of specified Nominal Accounts. Before producing a Quick Ratio between, say sales and purchases of a particular commodity, you will have to choose the Edit option from the

View Edit

options offered to you when you decide to look at the Quick ratio. This option allows you to specify the accounts you wish to examine by typing in their codes, SAGE will search for these and display the account names automatically. Having done that you can return and select the View option and produce a listing as shown in Fig. 2.5.2.

Account History will provide you with a complete list of all the transactions in that account. Choose the option and you will be asked for the range of accounts to be displayed. If you enter the account code for both the lower and the upper limits you will restrict the listing to one single account code. The choice is to display on the screen or print on the printer. Should you choose to display the histories of every nominal account you will get this with every account with the exception of the control accounts. The history of these is obtained through the Control Accounts reports option which is detailed next. If you choose the printer option you will receive a printout similar to that shown in Fig. 2.5.3. The codes used in the display in the two left hand columns are first the number of the transaction and secondly, under **Tp**, the type of transaction recorded:

PI — Purchase Invoice
SI — Sales Invoice
SC — Sales Credit Note
PC — Purchase Credit Note
SR — Sales Receipt
PP — Purchase Payment
BR — Bank Receipt
BP — Bank Payment
CR — Cash Receipt
CP — Cash Payment
JC — Journal Credit
JD — Journal Debit.

Choice of the Control Accounts option gives rise to another

```
PETER GOSLING                    Nominal Ledger Reports - Trial Balance.                Date : 010386
                                                                                        Page :    1
```

Ref.	Accounts Name	Debit	Credit
0100	Sierra	8543.00	
0101	Sierra depreciation		2345.00
0120	Metro	4111.00	
0121	Metro depreciation		1245.00
0130	Lada Estate	3789.00	
0131	Lada depreciation		1356.00
0140	Fixtures and Fittings	21986.00	
0200	Bank	31203.88	
0210	Cash	889.13	
0220	Debtor's Control	107615.81	
0320	Tax Control		4696.11
0330	Creditors Control		115281.93
0400	Directors Loan Account		11876.00
0410	Share Capital		9336.88
0420	Retained Profit		16749.19
1010	Hard Disk PC Sales		66457.32
1020	Twin Disk PC Sales		26508.98
1030	Single Disk PC Sales		17006.54
1110	Dot Matrix Printer Sales		6370.35
1120	NLQ Printer Sales		9655.77
1130	Daisy Wheel Printer Sales		5399.87
1210	Accounting S'ware Sales		17229.25
1220	Comms Software Sales		4937.88
1230	Bus. Risk S'ware Sales		889.00
1250	W.Proc. S'ware Sales		399.98
1310	Listing Paper Sales		6275.38
1320	Invoice Stationery Sales		539.00
1321	Statement Sales		771.88
1323	Other Document Sales		906.77
1330	Accessory Sales		690.10
1340	Floppy Disk Sales		800.54
1341	Micro Floppy Sales		341.86
2010	Hard Disk PC Purchases	37110.80	
2020	Twin Disk PC Purchases	22679.00	
2030	Single Disk PC Purchases	12299.80	
2110	D Matrix Printer Purch.	4113.69	
2120	NLQ Printer Purch.	6112.44	
2130	Daisy Wheel Printer Purch	6988.88	
2210	Accounting S'ware Purch	12713.00	
2220	Comms. S'ware Purchases	3799.00	
2230	Bus. Risk S'ware Purch	629.44	
2240	Data Base S'ware Purch	1983.89	
2250	W.Proc. S'ware Purchases	346.55	
2310	Listing Paper Purchases	5630.44	
2320	Invoice Stat. Purchases	300.22	
2330	Accessory Purchases	728.42	
2340	Floppy Disk Purchases	1177.98	
3010	Hotel Accomodation	3673.76	
3020	Entertainment	2806.98	
3030	Sundry Expenses	678.00	
3040	General Office Overheads	527.45	
3100	Petrol	1983.87	

PETER GOSLING

Nominal Ledger Reports - Trial Balance.

Ref.	Accounts Name	Debit	Credit
3150	Motor Expenses	795.00	
3210	Rent and Rates	4210.00	
3220	Gas and Electricity	927.00	
3230	Telephone Charges	1382.88	
3300	Directors Salaries	6000.00	
3310	Staff Salaries	5600.00	
3320	Casual Labour	952.90	
3400	Postage	849.87	
3410	Carriers	377.00	
3500	Equipment Rental	778.00	
3510	Building Repairs/Renewals	945.89	
3520	Stationery	198.76	
3600	Advertising	494.99	
3620	Sundries	132.86	
		328066.58	328066.58

Fig. 2.5.1.

```
PETER GOSLING          Management Reports - Quick Ratio.        Date : 010386
                                                                Page :    1

N/C    Account Name        Debit     Credit
       -----------------   --------  ----------
0210   Cash                  889.13
0220   Debtor's Control   107615.81
0200   Bank                31203.88
0320   Tax Control                     4696.11
0330   Creditors Control             115281.93
                                    ----------
                          19730.78
                                    ----------
```

Fig. 2.5.2.

PETER GOSLING   Sales Ledger Reports - Account History.   Date : 010386
                                                                                            Page :   1

Account : FORD   Ford Fish Factory,

No.	Tp	Date	Ref	Details	Value	Debit	Credit
73	SI	151185	o/bal	Micro System	2876.00 ‡	2876.00	
81	SI	261185	o/bal	Supplies	743.88	743.88	
90	SI	101285	o/bal	Software	1567.87 ‡	1567.87	
159	SI	010186	0045	Hard disk micros-3	15970.05		
160	SI	010186	0045	Two disk micros	6422.75 p		
				Amount Outstanding	1260.68		
161	SI	010186	0045	Diskettes	284.94 ‡	22677.74	
206	SR	290186	77689	Sales Receipt	21876.00		21876.00

Amount Outstanding   :   5989.49
Amount paid this period :   21876.00
Credit limit   :   25000.00
=============================

Fig. 2.5.3.

sub menu

> Debtor's Control
> Creditor's Control
> Bank Account
> Cash Account
> Tax Control
>
> Nominal Menu

Debtor's Control will search for and list all the transactions
with type of SI, SC or SR. Creditor's Control will list all the
transactions of types PI, PC or PP. the Bank Account option
will list all transactions of types BR, BP, SR and PP. The
Cash Account list, called Petty Cash in some systems, will
contain all transactions with types of CP or CR and the Tax
Control option will list all transactions of types SI, SC, PI,
PC, BR, BP, CR and CP.

2.6   Sales and Purchase Ledger Reports

The Sales Ledger Report sub menu is shown next.

> Account Names
> Account Balances
> Account History
> Statements
> Letters
> Report Generator
>
> Main Menu

The Purchase Ledger report sub menu is similar to that of the
Sales Ledger except that the fourth option becomes
Remittance Advice.

> Account Names
> Account Balances
> Account History
> Remittance Advice
> Letters
> Report Generator
>
> Main Menu

The first of these options will list the account identifiers together with the names, and addresses if required, of each of the companies on the ledger. An example of this is shown in Fig. 2.6.1. The second option will give the balances for each account together with the aged accounts as shown in Fig. 2.6.2 and 2.6.3. The Account History option will list the entries made to the account over the period for which the account has been open. If you perform a month-end routine when all paid accounts are cleared then the history will only be for the current month. A typical statement and remittance advice are shown in Fig. 2.6.4 and 2.6.5. The statements can be printed on continuous stationery available ready printed from Sagesoft. You will see that it has a remittance advice note printed alongside it. A remittance advice from the Purchase Ledger can be printed on blank paper or pre-printed stationery. For this purpose you are given the choice of printing your name and address at the top or not.

Letters which normally are used to 'chase' debtors are produced by the SAGE wordprocessor which lets you produce 'form' letters with spaces for the insertion of the appropriate data from the ledgers. You will usually find that you have the need to have three different letters. The first being of a 'soft' nature, the second more to the point and the third stating that legal action will be taken if the debt is not paid within, say, seven days.

The **Letters** option gives you the choice of sending letters to those who exceed their credit limit, have zero balances or who have not paid within a fixed number of days. The choices for that are 0, 30, 60, 90 or 120 days. Each of these options can be associated with a particular letter. The letter is generated from the Utilities Routines menu when you select the Text Editor choice. It is here that the letter is created, edited and saved. It is then selected for printing from the appropriate Report menu.

A typical letter of the second kind is shown on the screen in Fig. 2.6.6 and in its final printed form in Fig. 2.6.7.

To use the SAGE wordprocessor enter the name of the file you wish to edit or create — in this case it was called OVERDUE. The cursor can be moved around the screen

Axgro Foods Ltd.
13 Green Street
Alton on Sea

Bell Brothers Ltd
13, Brown Road,
Bradford,
W Yorks

Brown Bros. Ltd.
13, Bell Road,
Bradford,
W. Yorks
TW12 6 YB

C.B.Ltd.
34, Church Steet,
Durham.
DH3 4HL

Dun Distributors,
'Dunroamin'
34a Dunford Drive
Darlington,Co Durham.
D34 DH7

Ford Fish Factory,
23,Cod Place,
Haddock Hill,
Ealing.

Greens Greengrocery,
34,High Street,
High Handenhold,
Co Durham.
DH3 6WH

Jason Industries Ltd
Unit 12, Beech Ind Est
Freshwater
Somerset
WC3 5TF

Longlife Roof Felters,
12,The Mews,
South Kensington,
London,W3

Mild Steel Fabrications,
Unit 12,
Marquis of Granby Ind Est
Low Handenhold,
Co. Durham. DH4 4HH

Miles of Yarn Ltd.
3,Foot Yard,
Walton on Thames
London
SR9 7 WS

Mills Milliners,
16b,Trilby Lane,
Hatfield,
S12 4TF

Orange Electrics,
23,The Grove,
Leeds,
W Yorks.
WS34 2WD

Red Books Ltd.,
13,Marr Terrace,
Chopwell,
Newcastle on Tyne
NR17 3YH

Test Services Ltd
123 Green Street
Anytown
Yorks.

ZZPOP Ltd.
The Studio,
13.Green Street,
Consett,
Co Durham. DH3 4HS

Fig. 2.6.1.

PETER GOSLING

Sales Ledger Reports - Account Balances.

Date : 010386
Page : 1

A/C	Account Name	Turnover	Credit Limit	Balance	Current	30 days	60 Days	90 Days	Older
AXGRO	Axgro Foods Ltd. Alan Axgro (01 010 21010)	6909.04	15000.00	9497.29	0.00	6909.04	1144.25	68.00	1376.00
BBLL	Bell Brothers Ltd Peter Bell (0202 343432)	14135.23	15000.00	8722.48	0.00	8722.48	0.00	0.00	0.00
BROWN	Brown Bros. Ltd. Mike Brown (0202 567 876)	5898.98	15000.00	4495.89	0.00	3964.89	0.00	0.00	531.00
CBL	C.B.Ltd. Mr Bishop (091 284 8567)	7199.89	10000.00	4808.51	0.00	3499.51	0.00	0.00	1309.00
DUN	Dun Distributors, David Dun (0304 45678)	7179.67	2900.00	5617.55	0.00	0.00	675.88	2541.98	2399.69
FORD	Ford Fish Factory, Mr Whiting (01 345 6789)	22677.74	25000.00	5989.49	0.00	1545.62	1567.87	2876.00	0.00
GRBBN	Greens Greengrocery, Amber Green (091 345 6789)	966.00	5000.00	4925.13	0.00	966.00	339.25	3619.88	0.00

Code	Name								
LONG	Longlife Roof Felters, † Marley Tile (01 345 6789)	1969.87	2800.00	3522.98	0.00	1969.87	339.25	1211.86	0.00
MILD	Mild Steel Fabrications, Arthur Mild (0303 765 4567)	369.88	4000.00	1984.31	0.00	369.88	1035.95	578.48	0.00
MILES	Miles of Yarn Ltd. † Miles Parther (01 345 6789)	0.00	2700.00	7246.82	0.00	0.00	1567.85	0.00	5678.97
MILLS	Mills Milliners, † Andrew Capp (0207 567 8900)	17053.60	8000.00	25596.44	0.00	17053.60	1787.99	0.00	6754.85
ORANGE	Orange Electrics, † Arthur Orange (01234 5678)	5740.52	800.00	6350.17	0.00	5740.52	45.99	0.00	563.66
RED	Red Books Ltd., Ken Red (0207 508882)	6039.54	15000.00	11182.69	0.00	-3948.16	7164.87	0.00	7965.98
TEST	Test Services Ltd Annie Town (01 456 789)	230.00	7660.00	230.00	0.00	230.00	0.00	0.00	0.00
ZZPOP	ZZPOP Ltd. Pete (0207 67890)	4588.22	7500.00	7446.06	0.00	4588.22	821.30	2036.54	0.00
	Totals :	100958.18	136360.00	107615.81	0.00	51611.47	16490.45	12934.74	26579.15

Fig. 2.6.2.

PETER GOSLING
HIGHFIELD HOUSE
TOWER ROAD
WARFIELD, WORCS WA4 6TB

Brown Bros. Ltd.
13,Bell Road,
Bradford,
W.Yorks
TW12 6 YR

BROWN
010386
1

```
011185   o/bal   Micro System          531.00
040186   good1   Computer System
040186   good1   80 col Printer
040186   good1   Computer System
040186   good1   Plain cont. paper    3964.89


          0.00   3964.89    0.00    0.00    531.00
                                           4495.89
```

PETER GOSLING
HIGHFIELD HOUSE
TOWER ROAD
WARFIELD, WORCS WA4 6TB

Brown Bros. Ltd.
13,Bell Road,
Bradford,
W.Yorks
TW12 6 YR

BROWN
010386
1

```
011185   Micro System          531.00
040186   Computer System
040186   80 col Printer
040186   Computer System
040186   Plain cont. paper    3964.89


                               4495.89
```

Fig. 2.6.3.

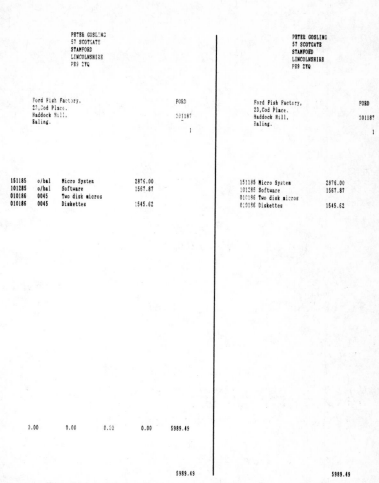

Fig. 2.6.4. Statement   Fig. 2.6.5. Remittance
                                              Advice

```
------Account-Name-------                    ------Date-£3------
-------Address-£1--------
-------Address-£2--------
-------Address-£3--------
-------Address-£4--------
```

Dear Sirs,

                    OVERDUE ACCOUNT £--Balance--

        With Reference to the above balance which is still outstanding
    on your account. May I remind you that our terms are strictly 30
    days nett and £---60-Day-- is more than 60 days overdue.

        Your remittance by return would be appreciated.

                        Yours faithfully,

                        Peter Gosling

                        Paul Walker,
                        COMPANY ACCOUNTANT.

Fig. 2.6.6.

Dun Distributors,   1st March 1986
'Dunroamin'
34a Dunford Drive
Darlington,Co Durham.
D34 DH7

Dear Sirs,

                    OVERDUE ACCOUNT £   5617.55

        With Reference to the above balance which is still outstanding
    on your account. May I remind you that our terms are strictly 30
    days nett and £   5617.55 is more than 60 days overdue.

        Your remittance by return would be appreciated.

                        Yours faithfully,

                        Peter Gosling

                        Paul Walker,
                        COMPANY ACCOUNTANT.

Fig. 2.6.7.

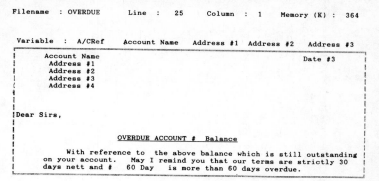

Filename : OVERDUE   Line : 25   Column : 1   Memory (K) : 364

Variable : A/CRef   Account Name   Address #1   Address #2   Address #3

```
         Account Name                                    Date #3
         Address #1
         Address #2
         Address #3
         Address #4


Dear Sirs,


                    OVERDUE ACCOUNT #  Balance

         With reference to  the above balance which is still outstanding
    on your account.   May I remind you that our terms are strictly 30
    days nett and #   60 Day   is more than 60 days overdue.
```

Fig. 2.6.8.

using the cursor keys as with any other wordprocessor and text typed in. When it comes to inserting data press the F4 key. This produces a list of the available variables displayed across the second line of the screen as shown in Fig. 2.6.8. Move the highlight to the field name you require to be inserted and press the **Return** key. This places the name of the field at the cursor position in the text.

2.7   Management reports, VAT analysis, audit trail, trial balance

By choosing the **Management Reports** option from the Main Menu you are presented with the following list of options

> Day Books
> Audit Trail
> VAT Return
> Monthly Accounts
> Budget Report
> Report Generator
>
> Main Menu

The first option gives you a further menu from which you

PETER GOSLING

Management Reports - Audit Trail.

Date : 010386
Page : 1

No.	Type	A/C	N/C	Dep	Details	Date	Inv.	Nett Amount	Tax Amount	TC	Paid	Date	Cheque	Amount Paid	N-AC	N-NC
100	SI	MILLS	0220	2	Stationery & Acces.	131285	o/bal	1787.99	0.00	T9	N			0.00	166	101
101	SI	ORANGE	0220	3	Supplies	151285	o/bal	45.99	0.00	T9	N			0.00	175	102
102	SI	RED	0220	1	Extra Workstation	151285	o/bal	5087.88	0.00	T9	N			0.00	103	103
103	SI	RED	0220	1	Supplies	151285	o/bal	2076.99	0.00	T9	N			0.00	172	104
104	SI	ZZPOP	0220	2	Supplies	151285	o/bal	821.30	0.00	T9	N			0.00	169	0
105	PI	ABLE	0330	10	Misc Hardware	031085	o/bal	15543.76	0.00	T9	N			0.00	106	106
106	PI	ABLE	0330	10	Electronic Comps.	021185	o/bal	287.87	0.00	T9	N			0.00	107	107
107	PI	ABLE	0330	10	Disk Units (3½b)	171285	o/bal	876.45	0.00	T9	N			0.00	183	108
108	PI	BAKER	0330	10	Cables & Misc.	171285	o/bal	456.76	0.00	T9	N			0.00	109	109
109	PI	BAKER	0330	10	Repairs	121285	o/bal	234.67	0.00	T9	N			0.00	199	110
110	PI	CHARLI	0330	10	Listing Paper	031185	o/bal	377.88	0.00	T9	N			0.00	111	111
111	PI	CHARLI	0330	10	Listing Paper	101185	o/bal	377.88	0.00	T9	N			0.00	112	112
112	PI	CHARLI	0330	10	Listing Paper	171185	o/bal	377.88	0.00	T9	N			0.00	113	113
113	PI	CHARLI	0330	10	Listing Paper	241185	o/bal	377.88	0.00	T9	N			0.00	114	114
114	PI	CHARLI	0330	10	Listing Paper	011285	o/bal	377.88	0.00	T9	N			0.00	115	115
115	PI	CHARLI	0330	10	Pre Printed Stat.	011285	o/bal	987.76	0.00	T9	N			0.00	116	116
116	PI	CHARLI	0330	10	Listing Paper	081285	o/bal	377.88	0.00	T9	N			0.00	191	117
117	PI	DELTA	0330	11	Computer Furniture	171185	o/bal	3987.88	0.00	T9	N			0.00	118	118
118	PI	DELTA	0330	11	Computer Furniture	171285	o/bal	5488.76	0.00	T9	N			0.00	186	119
119	PI	ECHO	0330	12	S/ware account Sept	011085	o/bal	3456.88	0.00	T9	N			0.00	120	120
120	PI	ECHO	0330	12	S/ware account Oct	011185	o/bal	456.88	0.00	T9	N			0.00	121	121
121	PI	ECHO	0330	12	S/ware account Nov	011285	o/bal	546.88	0.00	T9	N			0.00	193	122
122	PI	FOX	0330	11	Printers	011185	o/bal	5876.99	0.00	T9	N			0.00	123	123
123	PI	FOX	0330	11	Misc Supplies.	281285	o/bal	7099.18	0.00	T9	N			0.00	187	0
124	SI	AYGRO	1010	1	Hard Disk PC	010186	66001	4167.00	625.05	T1	N			0.00	125	129
125	SI	AYGRO	1110	2	Dot Matrix Printer	010186	66001	755.96	113.39	T1	N			0.00	126	132

					Description			Price	Amount					
126	SI	AXGRO	1210	3	SAGR Software	010186 66001		695.00	104.25	T1	N	0.00	127	134
127	SI	AXGRO	1310	1	Listing Paper	010186 66001		239.90	44.99	T1	N	0.00	128	139
128	SI	AXGRO	1320	2	2000 Pre Printed In	010186 66001		90.00	13.50	T1	N	0.00	201	148
129	SI	BELL	1010	1	Hard Disk PC	010186 66002	200186 8789	4167.00	625.05	T1	Y	4792.05	130	140
130	SI	BELL	1020	2	Twin Disk PC	010186 66002	200186 8789	2799.99	420.00	T1	N	620.70	131	151
131	SI	BELL	1030	3	Single Disk PC	010186 66002		1612.95	241.94	T1	N	0.00	132	152
132	SI	BELL	1110	1	Dot Matrix Printer	010186 66002		377.98	56.70	T1	N	0.00	133	141
133	SI	BELL	1130	2	Daisy Wheel Printer	010186 66002		599.99	90.00	T1	N	0.00	134	154
134	SI	BELL	1210	3	SAGR Software	010186 66002		695.00	104.25	T1	N	0.00	135	137
135	SI	BELL	1220	1	SAGR ChitChat Sw	010186 66002		145.00	21.75	T1	N	0.00	136	147
136	SI	BELL	1230	2	2xSAGR Options	010186 66002		399.00	59.85	T1	N	0.00	137	163
137	SI	BELL	1210	3	SAGRCOVRR	010186 66002		195.00	29.25	T1	N	0.00	138	142
138	SI	BELL	1250	1	Word Proc.S.Ware	010186 66002		99.99	15.00	T1	N	0.00	139	165
139	SI	BELL	1310	2	Listing Paper	010186 66002		1199.60	179.94	T1	N	0.00	202	143
140	SI	BROWN	1010	1	Computer System	040186 good1	200186 87654	4000.00	600.00	T1	N	1934.09	141	144
141	SI	BROWN	1110	1	80 col Printer	040186 good1		434.55	65.18	T1	N	0.00	142	153
142	SI	BROWN	1210	1	Computer System	040186 good1		495.00	74.25	T1	N	0.00	143	146
143	SI	BROWN	1310	1	Plain cont. paper	040186 good1		200.00	30.00	T1	N	0.00	204	171
144	SI	CBL	1010	2	Hard disk PC	060186 033	190186 k8990	4124.55	618.68	T1	N	3700.38	145	159
145	SI	CBL	1120	2	Printer	060186 033		412.77	61.92	T1	N	0.00	146	172
146	SI	CBL	1210	2	Accounts s.ware	060186 033		995.00	149.25	T1	N	0.00	147	155
147	SI	CBL	1220	2	Comms Pack	060186 033		399.00	59.85	T1	N	0.00	148	156
148	SI	CBL	1320	2	Pre printed inv.s	060186 033		200.00	30.00	T1	N	0.00	149	0
149	SI	CBL	1330	2	Accessories	060186 033		99.45	14.92	T1	N	0.00	150	158
150	SI	CBL	1340	2	Blank disks	060186 033		30.00	4.50	T1	N	0.00	203	161

Fig. 2.7.1.

PETER GOSLING   Management Reports - VAT Return.

Date from : 010186
to : 310186
Page : 1

Code : Rate :	T0 0.00	T1 15.00	T2 0.00	T3 0.00	T4 0.00	T5 0.00	T6 0.00	T7 0.00	T8 0.00	T9 0.00
Sales Tax Analysis										
Sales Invoices- Nett	0.00	81436.20	0.00	0.00	0.00	0.00	0.00	0.00	0.00	0.00
Sales Invoices- Tax	0.00	12342.31	0.00	0.00	0.00	0.00	0.00	0.00	0.00	0.00
Sales Credits- Nett	0.00	0.00	0.00	0.00	0.00	0.00	0.00	0.00	0.00	9987.70
Sales Credits- Tax	0.00	0.00	0.00	0.00	0.00	0.00	0.00	0.00	0.00	0.00
Purchase Tax Analysis										
Purchase Invoices- Nett	0.00	58881.67	0.00	0.00	0.00	0.00	0.00	0.00	0.00	0.00
Purchase Invoices- Tax	0.00	8832.26	0.00	0.00	0.00	0.00	0.00	0.00	0.00	0.00
Purchase Credits- Nett	0.00	0.00	0.00	0.00	0.00	0.00	0.00	0.00	0.00	0.00
Purchase Credits- Tax	0.00	0.00	0.00	0.00	0.00	0.00	0.00	0.00	0.00	0.00

Nominal Tax Analysis

Bank Receipts- Nett	0.00	0.00	0.00	0.00	0.00	0.00	0.00	0.00
Bank Receipts- Tax	0.00	0.00	0.00	0.00	0.00	0.00	0.00	0.00
Bank Payments- Nett	2438.00	0.00	6273.41	0.00	0.00	0.00	0.00	6299.90
Bank Payments- Tax	0.00	0.00	925.18	0.00	0.00	0.00	0.00	0.00
Cash Receipts- Nett	0.00	0.00	0.00	0.00	0.00	0.00	0.00	0.00
Cash Receipts- Tax	0.00	0.00	0.00	0.00	0.00	0.00	0.00	0.00
Cash Payments- Nett	66.98	0.00	1487.73	0.00	0.00	0.00	0.00	1800.00
Cash Payments- Tax	0.00	0.00	223.16	0.00	0.00	0.00	0.00	0.00
Journal Debits	0.00	0.00	0.00	0.00	0.00	0.00	0.00	0.00
.Journal Credits	0.00	0.00	0.00	0.00	0.00	0.00	0.00	0.00

Tax Analysis Summary

Inputs- Nett	2504.98	0.00	66642.81	0.00	0.00	0.00	0.00	6299.90
Inputs- Tax	0.00	0.00	9981.60	0.00	0.00	0.00	0.00	0.00
Outputs- Nett	0.00	0.00	81436.20	0.00	0.00	0.00	0.00	-8187.70
Outputs- Tax	0.00	0.00	12342.31	0.00	0.00	0.00	0.00	0.00

Fig. 2.7.2.

can choose the day book listing for various types of ledger entries.

Sales Invoices
Sales Credit Notes
Purchase Invoices
Purchase Credit Notes
Journal Entries

Management Menu

The audit trail will provide you with a list in order of all the entries between specified transaction numbers. A typical audit trail is shown in Fig. 2.7.1.

SAGE will compute your VAT liability, the third option on the Management Menu, and produce output as shown in Fig. 2.7.2.

The **Monthly Accounts** option gives you the ability to produce a Profit and Loss account and a Balance Sheet for the current month and the year to date. Before you print out the monthly accounts you will need to define those nominal accounts that are to be incorporated into these two reports. The Profit and Loss option gives rise to a menu giving the types of accounts to be incorporated. These are selected from the menu

Sales
Purchases
Direct Expenses
Overheads (1)
Overheads (2)
Overheads (3)

Monthly Menus

It is probably convenient for you to combine a number of nominal accounts together when producing the monthly accounts. For example, if you arrange for a set of consecutive account numbers to refer to items with some characteristic in common these can be combined into one single category. You may wish to combine purchases of a range of goods together under a general heading of PURCHASES. This can be done, but only if you have these accounts appearing consecutively in the nominal ledger. SAGE allows you to set a maximum of fifteen categories in this way. For example you enter sales accounts into a box as shown in Fig. 2.7.3.

The same thing is done for creating categories within the Balance Sheet, where the menu options are

> Fixed Assets
> Current Assets
> Liabilities
> Financed By
>
> Monthly Menus

Once this has been done you can print the Monthly Accounts, an example of which is shown in Fig. 2.7.4 and 2.7.5.

When you set up the Nominal accounts you were able, if you desired, to enter budget figures for each month of the year. Having done this you can compare the actual sales, purchases and other expenditure against the budgeted figure. By selecting the Budget Report option from the Management Reports menu you can produce a report for that month and for the year to date together with the amount by which the actual figure exceeds or falls short of the budget.

Category Heading	Low	High
PC Sales	1000	1099
UNUSED CATEGORY		
Printer Sales	1100	1199
UNUSED CATEGORY		
Software Sales	1200	1299
UNUSED CATEGORY		
Supply Sales -Stationery	1300	1329
-Accessories	1330	1339
-Diskettes	1340	1349
UNUSED CATEGORY		
UNUSED CATEGORY		
UNUSED CATEGORY		
UNUSED CATEGORY		
UNUSED CATEGORY		
UNUSED CATEGORY		
UNUSED CATEGORY		

Fig. 2.7.3.

PBTRB GOSLING   Management Reports - Profit & Loss Account.   Date : 010386
                                                                                         Page : 1

	This Month	Year to Date
Sales		
PC Sales	61549.84	109972.84
Printer Sales	9358.99	21425.99
Software Sales	12221.11	23456.11
Supply Sales - Stationery	3562.03	8493.03
- Accessories	345.10	690.10
- Diskettes	599.40	1142.40
	87636.47	165180.47
Purchases		
PC Purchases	36709.60	7089.60
Printer Purchases	8402.01	17215.01
Software Purchases	9764.88	19471.88
Supply Purch - Stationery	3022.43	5930.66
- Accessories	367.42	728.42
- Diskettes	615.33	1177.98
	58881.67	116613.55
Gross Profit	28754.80	Gross Profit 48566.92

```
Overheads
---------
Rent and Rates                      2105.00              4210.00
Salaries                            6299.90             12552.90
Travel Expense - Hotels             1777.76              3673.76
               - Entertainment      1319.98              2806.98
               - Sundries            333.00               678.00
Motor Expenses                      1386.87              2778.87
Office O'heads - Gas/Electric        489.00               927.00
               - Telephone           697.88              1382.88
               - Repair/Renew        487.89               945.89
               - Stationery           99.99               198.76
               - General             277.90               527.45
Postage/Delivery                     589.87              1226.87
Equipment Rental                     389.00               778.00
Advertising                          245.00               494.99
Sundries                              66.98               132.86
                                   --------             --------
                                   16566.02             33315.21
                                   --------             --------

Nett Profit    12188.78            Nett Profit          15251.71
               --------                                 --------
               ========                                 ========
```

Fig. 2.7.4.

PETER GOSLING   Management Reports - Balance Sheet.   Date : 010386
                                                                               Page :   1

	This Month	Year to Date
Fixed Assets		

Company Cars		11497.00
Fixtures and Fittings		21986.00

	0.00	33483.00
Current Assets		

Trade Debtors	36227.81	107615.81
Cash in Hand	22.13	889.13
Bank	46992.88	31203.88
	--------	---------
	83242.82	139708.82

Current Liabilities

VAT Liability	3340.11		4696.11	
Trade Creditors	67713.93		115281.93	
	--------		--------	
	71054.04		119978.04	
Nett Current Assets		12188.78		19730.78
		--------		--------
Total Assets less Current Liabilities		12188.78		53213.78
		========		========

Financed by

Directors Loans			11876.00
Share Capital			9336.88
Retained Profit			16749.19
Profit / Loss Account	12188.78		15251.71
	--------		--------
	12188.78		53213.78
	========		========

Fig. 2.7.5.

2.8   End of month and end of year procedures

At the end of each month you should run the reconfiguration routine found in the Utilities option chosen from the Main Menu. Apart from the fact that a regular end of the month 'cleanup' of the ledgers is good practice it will also prevent your disks becoming cluttered up with details of past months' completed transactions. Before running this part of the SAGE program you must take printed copies of the Sales, Purchase and Nominal Ledger reports, a copy of the Day Books, the Audit Trail and any other reports your auditor feels is necessary. In addition you should have a copy of the ledgers as they stand at the end of the month on a duplicate disk — SAGE recommend that you have two copies just to be on the safe side. Only then should you run the Reconfiguration routine. During this process all completed transactions are withdrawn from the files and a new opening Trial Balance is placed at the start of the Audit Trail.

At the end of the year you follow a similar procedure starting by printing out the Sales, Purchase and Nominal ledger reports together with the Audit Trail. Again take a copy of the ledgers as they stand at the end of the year and run the Reconfiguration routine. Then you can transfer the balances in both the Trading and Profit and Loss sections of the Trial Balance into a Nominal Account called 'Reserves'. This is done through the Journal. Finally print out the new Day Book and run the Reconfiguration program again to give a fresh set of ledgers ready for the new trading year.

3 Sage Accountant, Sage Accountant plus, Sage Financial Controller

3.1 The Report Generator

Any reports that have been described earlier in this book are in a format designed by Sagesoft and cannot be changed in any way. However, there is an easy way to produce reports and analyses tailored specifically to your particular needs. The SAGE Report Generator allows you to design your own reports and their layout using data from the various ledgers. Each report you create relates to a specific ledger and you cannot produce a report using data extracted from more than one ledger. You can see this from the report names if you list the directory. Sales Ledger reports are prefixed by the letters **SL**, Purchase ledger reports by **PL** and Nominal Ledger reports by **NL**. These prefixes are inserted by SAGE automatically, so that a Sales Ledger report named by you as ACCOUNTS is actually stored as SL__ACCOUNTS.REP.

As an example, select **Sales Ledger Reports** from the Main Menu. You are presented with a screen that has a box for you to enter the title of your report and space beneath giving the report title. Press Return to get to the next screen and you will see that you have the display shown in Fig. 3.1.1. Down

```
┌─────────────────────────────────────────────────────────────────┐
│ Report Generator          Accountant Plus        Date : 270187    │
└─────────────────────────────────────────────────────────────────┘


        Report Title :


Variables                      Selected Variables          Headings

Account Ref.              A :                    :
Account Name              B :                    :
Address 1                 C :                    :
Address 2                 D :                    :
Address 3                 E :                    :
Address 4                 F :                    :
Telephone Number          G :                    :
Contact Name              H :                    :
VAT Registration          I :                    :
Sort Code                 J :                    :
Last Invoice Date         K :                    :
First Trans. No.          L :                    :
Last  Trans. No.          M :                    :
Credit Limit              N :                    :
Turnover                  O :                    :
```

Fig. 3.1.1.

the left hand side you have a list of all the fields held, in this
case, on each record of the Sales Ledger.

Select the variables you wish to have included in your report
by moving the cursor to each one in turn by means of the up
and down arrow keys. You should notice that the sort code
that you may have used when setting up the account is listed
among the variables. It is only in the Report Generator that
this is made use of. Standard SAGE reports do not use it. The
same applies to a field at the end of the record that contains
the Department code. Select the order of variables by moving
the cursor in the second column up and down using the left
and right arrow keys. As the list of fields takes up more than
one display you can move through the list with the PgDn and
PgUp keys. The last two entries in the field list are of great
use. The first of these allows you to reserve a field for a
calculation and the second allows you to remove a field from
the report specification.

Make your selection by pressing the Return key. The name
of the field and its heading in the report are displayed
automatically in the second and third columns once the
selection has been made. The letters in the second column
indicate the order in which the columns will be printed across
each page of the report. Press Esc, and the cursor will move
into the third column in order for you to edit the report

```
| Report Generator          Accountant Plus          Date : 270187 |
```

Report Title :

Variables		Selected Variables		Headings
Account Ref.	A :	Account Name	:	Account Name
Account Name	B :	Credit Limit	:	Credit Lt.
Address 1	C :	Details	:	Details
Address 2	D :	Amount Nett	:	Nett Amount
Address 3	E :	Department	:	Dep.
Address 4	F :		:	
Telephone Number	G :		:	
Contact Name	H :		:	
VAT Registration	I :		:	
Sort Code	J :		:	
Last Invoice Date	K :		:	
First Trans. No.	L :		:	
Last Trans. No.	M :		:	
Credit Limit	N :		:	
Turnover	O :		:	

Fig. 3.1.2.

headings if you wish. Press the up-arrow key and you will be
able to edit the report title that will be displayed at the top of
each page of a multi-page report. A simple report layout is
shown in Fig. 3.1.2; it will list the sales accounts, their credit
limit, the details of each transaction, the nett amount of that
transaction and the department code.
Escape from this screen and the next screen is displayed giving
you the list of fields to be included in the report and the
number of characters to be taken up by each one — *see*
Fig. 3.1.3.

```
| Report Generator          Accountant Plus          Date : 270187 |
```

		Lth	Sort	Brk	Tot	CD	Selection Criteria
A	Account Name	25					
B	Credit Limit	11					
C	Details	19					
D	Amount – Nett	11					
E	Department	4					
F							
G							
H							
I							
J							
K							
L							
M							
N							
O							

Report Width   75

Fig. 3.1.3.

A specimen printout of this report for one account is shown in Fig. 3.1.4.

The columns beside the list of fields allow you to insert instructions to improve the layout of the report. For example, if you wish to use a field for a calculation but not display it you can reset the **Lth** entry for that field to zero.

You can sort on any fields by entering the codes **1A, 2A** or **3A** beside the field names indicating that you want the sort to be primarily on the 1A field, within that the 2A field and within that the 3A field. The **A** refers to an ascending sort. Replace the **A** with a **D** for a descending sort.

In the **Brk** column you can enter either **L** or **P** to create a line break or a page break. A break will produce a subtotal of totalled fields. A field to be totalled is indicated by a **Y** inserted in the **Tot** column. The fifth column, **CD**, can have either a **C** or a **D** entered if required. If a **C** is entered in this column then only amounts less than zero (i.e. credits) will be displayed. If a **D** is entered then only amounts greater than or equal to zero are displayed (i.e. debits).

The column with the heading **Selection Criteria** allows you to print selectively from the ledger. You can print all records where the invoice number is in a specified range, or the dates are before a particular date using a series of logical tests involving the following operators

=	Equal to	**AND**	Logical AND
!=	Not equal to	**OR**	Logical OR
<	Less than		
>	Greater than		
<=	Less than or equal to		
>=	Greater than or equal to		

The usual DOS-type wildcards can be used so that * stands for a string of characters of any type and ? for a single character. Text can be compared if it is enclosed in quotation marks.

In order to perform arithmetic on the contents of any field, or fields, calculation fields can be included having been allowed space when the report was defined. The usual arithmetic operators (+, −, * and /) as well as brackets can

PETER GOSLING

Account details

Account Name	Credit Lt.	Details	Nett Amount	Dep.
Axgro Foods Ltd.	15000.00	Micro System	4876.00	1
Axgro Foods Ltd.	15000.00	Supplies	567.00	1
Axgro Foods Ltd.	15000.00	Software	1144.25	1
Axgro Foods Ltd.	15000.00	Hard Disk PC	4167.00	1
Axgro Foods Ltd.	15000.00	Dot Matrix Printer	755.96	2
Axgro Foods Ltd.	15000.00	SAGE Software	695.00	3
Axgro Foods Ltd.	15000.00	Listing Paper	299.90	1
Axgro Foods Ltd.	15000.00	2000 Pre Printed In	90.00	2
Axgro Foods Ltd.	15000.00	Sales Receipt	0.00	1

Fig. 3.1.4.

be used. Together with these there are some special SAGE
operators available. These are

R — the date of the report
S — the lower date range as defined when the report is
    printed.
T — the upper date range as defined when the report was
    printed.
P — a variable that can have one of three values:

P = 1   if the transaction type is SI, PC, BR or CR
P = −1   if the transaction type is SC, PI, BP or CP
P = 0   if the transaction type is JD or JC

A selection criterion should be prefixed by a = sign, < or >
in order to state that the selection is made on the contents of
that field being equal to, less than or greater than the
expression following.

If, for example, you wished to print an extract from a
ledger for all transactions between a pair of dates then you
would select the date field and in the Selection Criterion space
beside it enter an instruction such as

> = 010188 AND < 010288

so that the record details are only printed if the date is greater
than or equal to 1 January 1988 and less than 1 February
1988 (i.e. during the month of January 1988). If you wanted
to perform a calculation using data from a particular field and
then display the answer in the report you must reserve an
empty space for the calculation field. Then you must mark the
field as being a Calculation Field by using the last entry but
one in the Field description column. You can then enter the
calculation instructions such as

C * .15

meaning that the contents of this field must contain the result
of multiplying the contents of field C by .15. The heading for
this field can, of course, be supplied by you.

4 Sage Accountant Plus, Sage Financial Controller

4.1 Stock control, stock valuation, re-order levels and stock movement audit trail, price lists

Because SAGE provides links between the invoicing module and the stock control module you are able to relate invoices directly to stock levels as you create the invoice. On choosing **Stock Control** from the Main Menu you are presented with the following options:

> Update Stock Details
> Category Names
> Adjustments In
> Adjustments Out
> Month End
> Year End
> Stock Reports
>
> Main Menu

the first selection provides you with a screen enabling you to amend any of the following items:

Stock Code *
Description *
Category *
Selling Price *
Cost Price
Unit of Sale *
Reorder level *
Reorder quantity *
Three rates of discount *
Nominal Ledger code *
Department *
VAT code *
Supplier **
Part Reference *
Location *

The SAGE program will alter the following stock parameters.
You cannot alter them from a screen. They will only be
changed if you make a stock transaction, such as creating an
invoice or receiving items into stock. The parameters are:

Quantity in stock
Stock on order
Stock allocated
Quantity sold in the month and so far this year (Year to Date)
Sales value for the month and Year to Date
Date of last sale
Date of last purchase

When you start the stock control system you will have a
screenful of empty data boxes that you can fill in with the
initial stock details relating to the items marked with * on the
list above. The item marked **, Supplier, will require the code
used for that supplier as entered in the Purchase Ledger. If
you enter a non-existent code SAGE will reject it. This applies
to any code that is used throughout SAGE. It will not accept
unrecognizable codes, or dates for that matter.

 There is no question of entering opening balances as there is
with the ledgers. Obviously you will have to place the initial

stock values on the appropriate nominal ledger account in the first instance, however.

When you have completed your entry onto the screen as with all SAGE entries you are given the choice

Post Abandon Edit

when you press Esc.

You can only delete an item from the stock list if there is no stock in hand. If this is so press Esc and you will be given the choice of

Post Abandon Delete

Select the last of these and the item will be deleted from the stock list.

Ninety stock categories are allowed to be used in SAGE Stock Control. When the **Category Names** option is chosen you are presented with a blank list that you can edit so that it looks, for example, as shown in Fig. 4.1.1.

The **Adjustments In** option from the menu allows you to enter details of stock that has been received. You will need to enter the stock code reference, the unit cost price, the quantity and an order number reference. The unit cost, which can be different from the previous unit cost of that item, will be used for the calculation of stock value. The **Adjustments Out** option requires the same information. When making an

```
| Category Names              Accountant Plus              Date : 270187  |

        Category Name   1    | Hard Disk PC
        Category Name   2    | Twin Disk PC
        Category Name   3    | Single Disk PC
        Category Name   4    | Dot Matrix Printers
        Category Name   5    | NLQ Printers
        Category Name   6    | Daisy Wheel Printers
        Category Name   7    | Accounting Software
        Category Name   8    | Communications Software
        Category Name   9    | Business Risk Software
        Category Name  10    | Word Processing Software
        Category Name  11    | Listing Paper
        Category Name  12    | Invoice Stationery
        Category Name  13    | Statements
        Category Name  15    | Other Documents
        Category Name  16    | Floppy Disks
```

Fig. 4.1.1.

```
PETER GOSLING                    Stock Reports - Stock Valuation.                    Date : 010386
                                                                                     Page :    1

Category :  1 : Hard Disk PC
----------------------------

                                    Quantity  Average     Stock      Selling   Expected
     Stock Code    Stock Description In Stock  Unit Cost   Value      Price     Sales

     PC1   B&W 10MB Hard Disk PC       11.00   2445.45    26900.00   3000.00   33000.00
     PC2   Colour 10MB Hard Disk PC     8.00   3000.00    24000.00   3600.00   28800.00
     PC3   B&W 20MB Hard Disk PC        3.00   2950.00     8850.00   3500.00   10500.00
     PC4   Colour 20MB Hard Disk PC     4.00   3550.00    14200.00   4100.00   16400.00
                                                         ---------            ---------
                                               Total :   73950.00            88700.00

Category :  2 : Twin Disk PC
----------------------------

     PC5   B&W Twin Disk PC             5.00   2000.00    10000.00   2500.00   12500.00
     PC6   Colour Twin Disk PC          6.00   2650.00    15900.00   3100.00   18600.00
                                                         ---------            ---------
                                               Total :   25900.00            31100.00
```

PETER GOSLING   Stock Reports - Stock Valuation.   Date : 010386
                                                                                     Page : 2

Category Value of Stock Totals

Category 1 : Hard Disk PC   :   73950.00   Category 2 : Twin Disk PC   :   25900.00

Grand Total Value of Stock :   ::::::::::
                                99850.00
                                ::::::::::

Fig. 4.1.2.

PRTRR COSLING   Stock Reports - Stock History.

Category : 1 : Hard Disk PC

Stock Code : PC1   : B&W 10MB Hard Disk PC

Type	Date	Ref.	Details	Quantity	Qty Used	Cost Pr.	Sale Pr.
AI	050686	O/BAL	Opening Stock	8.00	0.00		2500.00
MI	090686		Stock Transfer	3.00	0.00		2300.00

Quantity In stock   : 11.00
Quantity On Order   : 2.00
Quantity Allocated : 0.00

Stock Code : PC2   : Colour 10MB Hard Disk PC

Type	Date	Ref.	Details	Quantity	Qty Used	Cost Pr.	Sale Pr.
AI	050686	O/BAL	Opening Stock	8.00	0.00		3000.00

Quantity In stock   : 8.00
Quantity On Order   : 0.00
Quantity Allocated : 0.00

```
Stock Code : PC3           : B&W 20MB Hard Disk PC

Type Date  Ref.    Details        Quantity Qty Used Cost Pr. Sale Pr.
----------------------------------------------------------------------
AI 050686 O/BAL  Opening Stock      3.00     0.00   2950.00

Quantity In stock   :   3.00
Quantity On Order   :   2.00
Quantity Allocated  :   0.00
======================================================================


Stock Code : PC4           : Colour 20MB Hard Disk PC

Type Date  Ref.    Details        Quantity Qty Used Cost Pr. Sale Pr.
----------------------------------------------------------------------
AI 050686 O/BAL  Opening Stock      4.00     0.00   3550.00

Quantity In stock   :   4.00
Quantity On Order   :   0.00
Quantity Allocated  :   0.00
======================================================================
```

Fig. 4.1.3.

PETER GOSLING   Stock Reports - Stock Details.

Date : 010386
Page :   1

Category : 1 : Hard Disk PC

Stock Code   : PC1
Stock Desc.   : B&W 10MB Hard Disk PC
Department Code : 1
Tax Code   : T1
Nominal Code   : 1010
Re-Order Level :   5.00
Re-Order Qty.   :   2.00

In-Stock   :   11.00
On-Order   :   2.00
Allocated   :   0.00
Bin Location   :
Discount Rate A :   0.00
Discount Rate B :   5.00
Discount Rate C :   10.00

Units of Sale   : each
Sup. Part Ref. : 900/0001
Supplier Code   : FOX
Purchase Price : 2300.00
Selling Price   : 3000.00
Date Last Pur. :
Date Last Sale :

Stock Code   : PC2
Stock Desc.   : Colour 10MB Hard Disk PC
Department Code : 1
Tax Code   : T1
Nominal Code   : 1010
Re-Order Level :   6.00
Re-Order Qty.   :   3.00

In-Stock   :   8.00
On-Order   :   0.00
Allocated   :   0.00
Bin Location   :
Discount Rate A :   0.00
Discount Rate B :   5.00
Discount Rate C :   10.00

Units of Sale   : each
Sup. Part Ref. : 900/0002
Supplier Code   : FOX
Purchase Price : 3000.00
Selling Price   : 3600.00
Date Last Pur. :
Date Last Sale :

Stock Code   : PC3
Stock Desc.   : B&W 20MB Hard Disk PC
Department Code : 1
Tax Code   : T1
Nominal Code   : 1010
Re-Order Level : 5.00
Re-Order Qty.   : 2.00

In-Stock   : 3.00
On-Order   : 2.00
Allocated   : 0.00
Bin Location   :
Discount Rate A : 0.00
Discount Rate B : 5.00
Discount Rate C : 10.00

Units of Sale   : each
Sup. Part Ref. : 900/0003
Supplier Code   : FOX
Purchase Price : 2950.00
Selling Price : 3500.00
Date Last Pur. :
Date Last Sale :

Stock Code   : PC4
Stock Desc.   : Colour 20MB Hard Disk PC
Department Code : 1
Tax Code   : T1
Nominal Code   : 1010
Re-Order Level : 5.00
Re-Order Qty.   : 2.00

In-Stock   : 4.00
On-Order   : 0.00
Allocated   : 0.00
Bin Location   :
Discount Rate A : 0.00
Discount Rate B : 5.00
Discount Rate C : 10.00

Units of Sale   : each
Sup. Part Ref. : 900/0004
Supplier Code   : FOX
Purchase Price : 3550.00
Selling Price : 4100.00
Date Last Pur. :
Date Last Sale :

Fig. 4.1.4

adjustment out the cost price will be shown as zero, but this does not affect the cost price as shown on the stock ledger.

If you are using FINANCIAL CONTROLLER you will find that there is an extra option on the menu as shown here:

Update Stock Details
Category Names
Adjustments In
Adjustments Out
Stock Transfer
Month End
Year End
Stock Reports

Main Menu

The **Stock Transfer** option allows you to make up a new stock item from separate components that are held in stock. This is because FINANCIAL CONTROLLER allows you to perform a parts 'explosion' so that each separate stock item can be broken down into its components. For example an engine comprises a cylinder block, cylinder head, sump, carburettor, electrics, petrol pump and so on. In the ACCOUNTANT PLUS program an engine has to be kept on stock as just an engine, but in FINANCIAL CONTROLLER the engine can be split up into its component parts each separately bought in, stored and valued as required. This means that far more detailed records can be kept.

In order to have an up-to-date report on the value of the stock currently choose the **Stock Reports** option from the menu shown on page 59. This will give you the following menu:

Stock Details
Stock History
Stock Valuation
Stock Profit MTH
Stock Profit YTD
Re-Order Level
Report Generator

Stock Menu

PETER GOSLING

Stock Reports - Stock Profit YTD.

Date : 010386
Page : 1 ..

Stock Code	Description	Quantity Sold	Sales Value	Cost Of Sales	Profit	Profit (%)
AC5	Integrated Accounts	6.00	7770.00	6750.00	1020.00	15.11
PT1	80 Column Printer	5.00	1500.00	1100.00	400.00	36.36
PT2	132 Column Printer	4.00	1600.00	1280.00	320.00	25.00
PT3	220 Column Printer	4.00	2400.00	2080.00	320.00	15.38
PT4	Laser Printer	3.00	10500.00	8250.00	2250.00	27.27
PT5	Daisy Wheel Printer	2.00	3000.00	2100.00	900.00	42.86
ST1	Preprint Statements 1000 Sheet	1.00	25.00	18.00	7.00	38.89
	Totals :		26795.00	21578.00	5217.00	24.18

Fig. 4.1.5.

PETER GOSLING

Stock Reports - Re-Order Level.

Stock Code	Description	Quantity In Stock	Quantity Allocate	Quantity On-Order	Re-Order Level	Re-Order Quantity	Purchase Price	P/C
AC1	IBM Accountant software	5.00	0.00	2.00	10.00	20.00	450.00	SAGE
AC2	ACT Accountant Software	5.00	0.00	2.00	10.00	20.00	450.00	SAGE
AC3	MSDOS Accountant Software	4.00	0.00	5.00	10.00	20.00	450.00	SAGE
AC5	Integrated Accounts	4.00	0.00	0.00	5.00	10.00	1125.00	SAGE
DK1	10 x 5.25" DS DD Disks	30.00	0.00	0.00	30.00	10.00	12.00	ECHO
DK2	10 x 5.25" DS SD Disks	20.00	0.00	0.00	30.00	10.00	20.00	ECHO
DK3	10 x 5.25" SS DD Disks	30.00	0.00	0.00	30.00	10.00	11.00	ECHO
DK5	10 x 5.25" DS DD 96tpi Disks	10.00	0.00	0.00	30.00	10.00	27.00	ECHO
PC10MB	10mb unit for PC	2.00	0.00	0.00	5.00	5.00	500.00	FOX
PC20MB	20mb unit for PC	3.00	0.00	0.00	5.00	5.00	950.00	FOX
PC3	B&W 20MB Hard Disk PC	3.00	0.00	2.00	5.00	2.00	2950.00	FOX
PC4	Colour 20MB Hard Disk PC	4.00	0.00	0.00	5.00	2.00	3550.00	FOX
PC5	B&W Twin Disk PC	5.00	0.00	2.00	5.00	2.00	2000.00	FOX
PC6	Colour Twin Disk PC	6.00	0.00	0.00	6.00	2.00	2650.00	FOX
PC8	Colour Single Disk PC	10.00	0.00	0.00	5.00	4.00	1950.00	FOX
PCBASE	PC base unit	4.00	0.00	0.00	5.00	5.00	1150.00	FOX
PCBWMON	Black and white monitor	1.00	0.00	0.00	5.00	5.00	0.00	FOX
PCCOLMON	PC colour monitor	4.00	0.00	0.00	5.00	5.00	700.00	FOX
PCKEY	PC keyboard	4.00	0.00	0.00	5.00	5.00	650.00	FOX
PT1	80 Column Printer	3.00	0.00	0.00	4.00	10.00	220.00	ABLE
PT3	220 Column Printer	3.00	0.00	0.00	3.00	5.00	520.00	ABLE
PT4	Laser Printer	2.00	0.00	0.00	4.00	5.00	2750.00	ABLE
PT5	Daisy Wheel Printer	2.00	0.00	0.00	2.00	1.00	1050.00	ABLE
SS1	Spreadsheet Software	5.00	0.00	0.00	5.00	2.00	200.00	SAGE

Fig. 4.1.6.

The **Stock Valuation** option will give you a report similar to the type shown in Fig. 4.1.2.

The Stock History report will record the movement of each item of stock as shown in Fig. 4.1.3. With this report there

PETER GOSLING

Price List at 1st March 1986

Date : 010386
Page :   1

Category Name	Stock Code	Stock Description	Sale Price
Accounting Software	AC1	IBM Accountant software	495.00
Accounting Software	AC2	ACT Accountant Software	495.00
Accounting Software	AC3	MSDOS Accountant Software	495.00
Accounting Software	AC4	Accountant Plus (MSDOS)	695.00
Accounting Software	AC5	Integrated Accounts	1295.00
Business Risk Software	SS1	Spreadsheet Software	375.00
Business Risk Software	SS2	Risk Analysis Software	295.00
Communication Software	CM1	Electronic Mail	70.00
Communication Software	CM2	Viewdata Software	70.00
Communication Software	CM3	File Transfer Software	95.00
Daisy Wheel Printers	PT5	Daisy Wheel Printer	1500.00
Dot Matrix Printers	PT1	80 Column Printer	300.00
Dot Matrix Printers	PT2	132 Column Printer	400.00
Dot Matrix Printers	PT3	220 Column Printer	600.00
Floppy Disks	DK1	10 x 5.25" DS DD Disks	25.00
Floppy Disks	DK2	10 x 5.25" DS SD Disks	22.50
Floppy Disks	DK3	10 x 5.25" SS DD Disks	22.50
Floppy Disks	DK4	10 x 5.25" SS SD Disks	20.00
Floppy Disks	DK5	10 x 5.25" DS DD 96tpi Disks	30.00
Floppy Disks	DK6	10 x 5.25" SS DD 96tpi Disks	25.00
Hard Disk PC	PC1	B&W 10MB Hard Disk PC	3000.00
Hard Disk PC	PC2	Colour 10MB Hard Disk PC	3600.00
Hard Disk PC	PC3	B&W 20MB Hard Disk PC	3500.00
Hard Disk PC	PC4	Colour 20MB Hard Disk PC	4100.00
Invoice Stationery	IS1	Preprinted Invoices 1000 Sheet	25.00
Invoice Stationery	IS2	Preprinted Invoices 1000 Sheet	22.50
Invoice Stationery	IS3	Plain Invoices 1000 Sheets	15.00
Invoice Stationery	IS4	Plain Invoices 2000 Sheets	17.00
Listing Paper	LP1	1 Part plain, box 2000 Sheets	12.00
Listing Paper	LP2	1 Part ruled, box 2000 Sheets	12.00
Listing Paper	LP3	2 Part plain, box 1000 Sheets	12.00
Listing Paper	LP4	2 Part ruled, box 1000 Sheets	12.00
Listing Paper	LP5	3 Part plain, box 750 Sheets	12.00
Listing Paper	LP6	4 Part ruled, box 500 Sheets	12.00
Micro Floppy Disks	DK7	10 x 3.25" SS Auto Shutter	20.00
Micro Floppy Disks	DK8	10 x 3.25" DS DD Disks	23.00
NLQ Printers	PT4	Laser Printer	3500.00
Other Documents	ST5	Payslips, box 1000 Sheets	15.00
Other Documents	ST6	Payslips, box 2000 Sheets	15.00
PC Components	PC10MB	10mb unit for PC	0.00
PC Components	PC20MB	20mb unit for PC	0.00
PC Components	PCBASE	PC base unit	0.00
PC Components	PCBWMON	Black and white monitor	0.00
PC Components	PCCOLMON	PC colour monitor	0.00
PC Components	PCKEY	PC keyboard	0.00
Single Disk PC	PC7	B&W Single Disk PC	2000.00
Single Disk PC	PC8	Colour Single Disk PC	2600.00
Statements	ST1	Preprint Statements 1000 Sheet	25.00
Statements	ST2	Preprint Statements 1000 Sheet	25.00
Statements	ST3	Plain Statements 2000 Sheets	15.00

Fig. 4.1.7.

are six transaction types specific to the Stock Ledger. They are

AI	Adjustment In
AO	Adjustment Out
MI	Movement In
MO	Movement Out
GI	Goods In
GO	Goods Out

From this report you will be able to see the way in which any particular stock item has been moving so that a Stock Audit Trail is available.

If the Stock Details selection is made a full report on the state of a set of stock items. An example of this is shown in Fig. 4.1.4.

The Stock Profits report, this time by stock code, either for the current month or for the Year To Date will look as shown in Fig. 4.1.5.

The previous four reports will be available as screen displays, printouts or a disk file. The Re-Order Level report is always given as a printed report of all stock items that are below the re-order level, or are at the re-order level. A typical printed report of this type is shown in Fig. 4.1.6.

The report generator used in conjunction with the Stock files can be used to produce a current price list by printing the category, stock number, stock description and sale price. If you allot the sort code 1A to the category and the sort code 2A to the stock number you will get a report of the type shown in Fig. 4.1.7.

4.2   Invoicing, designing an invoice, integrating invoices with stock files

The invoicing routines available with SAGE, which also enable you to produce credit notes, allow you to integrate your invoices with the Sales Ledger and the Stock files only if you require. If you are using FINANCIAL CONTROLLER then the Sales Order Processing routine will produce the invoices. This is described in detail in Chapter 5.

The creation of an invoice or credit note falls into three

parts. The first of these is the general part consisting of the customer name and address, and delivery address if required. The second part is the detail part where every item to be included on the invoice is recorded. There is one separate screen for each item. The final part is the 'footing' of the invoice where the total for the invoice is displayed together with any carriage costs, discounts and general notes.

First of all select **Invoice Production** from the Main Menu. This will display the following set of options.

> Enter Invoices
> Enter Credit Notes
> Invoice Index
> Invoice Print
> Update Ledgers
> Invoice Deletion
>
> Main Menu

Choose the **Enter Invoice** option and the first screen is displayed as shown in Fig. 4.2.1.

You can move around this screen by means of the arrow keys in order to edit entries. The invoice number is kept up to date by the SAGE system and starts at 1. The date on the invoice is the current date and both of these can be changed if you wish. The Sales Ref field is the Sales Ledger code for that

```
┌──────────────────────────────────────────────────────────────────────────┐
│  Enter Invoices            Accountant Plus              Date : 270187  │
└──────────────────────────────────────────────────────────────────────────┘

Invoice No      :


Date            :
Sales Ref       :


Customer Name   :                        Order No.       :    0
Customer Address:                        Customer Order No:
           "    :
           "    :
           "    :

Telephone       :
                                         Total Nett    :    0.00
Delivery Name   :                        Total Tax     :    0.00
Delivery Address:
           "    :                        Total Gross   :    0.00
           "    :
           "    :                        Early Payment :    0.00
```

Fig. 4.2.1.

customer. If the customer is not on your Sales Ledger then press the down arrow key to move to the name and address field, which can be filled in manually. If the customer has an account then the account details are automatically retrieved and displayed. If the delivery address is the same as the customer address then -**AS INVOICED**- appears in the delivery address section. The order number is for you to use as your system dictates and the customer order number can be filled in below it. The box at the bottom right of the screen will only display zeros at this point. It is only when the invoice is complete that a significant entry is shown. At this point you can go no further until you press the PgDn key. This takes you to the first of the detail screens (*see* Fig. 4.2.2).

As with the first screen this one can be used to select items from stock, details of which will be displayed automatically, or may be entered manually. If there is no stock code to be entered then by pressing the down arrow key you are allowed to enter the item details manually. Two comment lines under the stock description make it possible for you to expand the description over three lines. If you are entering the details from the Stock List then a message will be displayed should the item not be in stock or if there is not sufficient to cover the order. The tax code can be changed by you, but the tax value cannot be changed, except through the Utilities. You should note that the number of decimal places in the Units

```
┌─────────────────────────────────────────────────────────────────────┐
│  Enter Invoices          Accountant Plus            Date : 270187  │
│                                                                       │
│ Invoice No.      :                     Total Nett    :    0.00       │
│ Customer         :                     Total Tax     :    0.00       │
│ Item No.         :                     Total Gross   :    0.00       │
│                                                                       │
│ Stock Code       :                                                    │
│ Description      :                                                    │
│ Comment 1        :                                                    │
│ Comment 2        :                                                    │
│                                                                       │
│                                                                       │
│ Quantity         :    0.00                                            │
│ Units            :                                                    │
│ Unit Price       :    0.00                                            │
│                                                                       │
│ Discount%        :          0.00       Cost         :    0.00        │
│ Tax Code         :                     Discount     :    0.00        │
│ Tax Value%       :          0.00       Subtotal     :    0.00        │
│ Nominal Code     :                                  ---------        │
│ Department       : 0                   TOTAL        :    0.00        │
└─────────────────────────────────────────────────────────────────────┘
```

Fig. 4.2.2.

and Unit Price fields have to be set up through the INSTALL routine described in the first chapter of this Companion.

The Nominal Code must be entered if you are going to update the ledgers after you have printed the invoice. By pressing the down arrow key you move to a clear detail screen for entry of the next invoice item. This is completed in the same way and you continue until all the items for that invoice have been entered. Finally press the PgDn key to take you on to the third type of invoice screen. This one deals with the 'footings' of the invoice so that you can enter carriage and packing details, which themselves can be transferred through their own nominal codes and tax codes through to the appropriate ledgers.

You should note, however, that if you are going to post each item on the invoice separately then the nominal codes have to be entered for each item and not on the 'footings' screen. If, on the other hand, you are intending to post the entire invoice as a single transaction then you enter a nominal code only on the 'footings' screen.

Credit notes are entered in exactly the same way as invoices.

Once you have created an invoice it will be stored away ready for printing and posting and you can display the current batch of invoices by choosing the Invoice Index option from the Invoice Production menu. It will show whether posting and/or printing has taken place as shown in Fig. 4.2.3.

Choose Invoice Print from the menu and one or more of

Invoice Index			Accountant Plus		Date : 010386
Inv/Crd	No.	Date	Customer Name	Printed	Posted
INVOICE	1	280286	Jaycessories	Yes	Yes
INVOICE	2	280286	M & B Supplies	Yes	Yes
INVOICE	3	010386	Fortune Accessories	Yes	
CREDIT	4	010386	Blue Line Cafe		
INVOICE	5	010386	Jason Industries Ltd	Yes	

Press   ESC   to finish.   RETURN to continue

Fig. 4.2.3.

the invoices will be printed in the form shown in Fig. 4.2.4. Notice how they do not need pre-printed invoice forms as the invoice layout file, INVOICE.LYT, defines the form and content of the invoice. Should you want to alter this then you can do so by using the text editor. You will have to do this in any case before you send out your first invoice since the file

```
*********************************
******      Peter Gosling      *******
*********************************
```

```
                                          Highfield House
                                          Tower Road
                                          Warfield, Worcs WA4 6TR
                                          Telephone: 0123 45678


                                          VAT No.: 123 4567 89

                 Jason Industries Ltd     Account Ref.    JASON
                 Unit 12, Beech Ind Est
                 Freshwater               Invoice Date    01/03/86
                 Somerset
                 WL3 5TF                   Invoice No.       5
```

QUANTITY	DETAILS	DISC	NETT PRICE	VAT
1.00	B&W 20MB Hard Disk PC	0.00	3500.00	525.00
2.00	10 x 5.25" DS SD Disks	0.00	45.00	6.75

Total Nett	3545.00
Packing	0.00
VAT	531.75
TOTAL	4076.75

YOUR ORDER NO. : 78787

DELIVERY ADDRESS : ------ AS INVOICED ------

Fig. 4.2.4.

called INVOICE.LYT provided by SAGESOFT bears their own name and address and other details that will need to be amended by you before using the invoicing routine.

Note: An invoice can only be printed once: if you require a copy invoice you may print a copy by going back to the Enter Invoice routine, as if you were going to create a new one. Enter the number of the invoice to be reprinted and its details will be displayed on the screen. Press **Esc** and Post the invoice. Then you can print it again through the Invoice Print routine. The other alternative is to use two part stationery and print two at once.

If you choose the Invoice Deletion option from the menu you will be able to dispose of any invoices once they have been both posted and printed. Should you attempt to delete an invoice that has not been either posted or printed then SAGE will inform you. You may want to delete an invoice before posting if by some mischance you have made an error in its creation.

5   Sage Financial Controller

5.1   Stock explosion and stock transfer

SAGE FINANCIAL CONTROLLER adds a number of extra features onto the other three programs. The first of these is the Stock explosion. This option is one of the reports chosen from the Stock Reports menu, shown on page 68.

When any stock item is made up of a series of discrete components, each of which is retained individually in stock, then a stock — or parts — explosion will list each stock item and its constituents as shown in Fig. 5.1.1.

The details of the assembly for any stock item are created by the Update Stock Details option from the Stock Control menu. This screen is slightly different for the FINANCIAL CONTROLLER program from that already described. The details required to be entered on the screen are the same as described on page 60 but with the addition of a field called **Make Up**. If you position the cursor on that field and press the **Return** key the number, initially zero, will display the number of complete items that can be created from the components held in stock.

So that you can specify the components required to make a finished stock item press the PgDn key and a new screen will be displayed. This screen allows you to enter the stock code

```
PETER GOSLING              Stock Reports - Stock Explosion.                    Date : 010386
                                                                              Page :      1

Category : 1    Name : Hard Disk PC
------------------------------------------------------------------------------

PC1            B&W 10MB Hard Disk PC              Location    Quantity
                                                 ----------  --------
PC10MB         10mb unit for PC                                  1.00
PCBASE         PC base unit                                      1.00
PCBWMON        Black and white monitor                           1.00
PCKEY          PC keyboard                                       1.00

PC2            Colour 10MB Hard Disk PC          Location    Quantity
                                                 ----------  --------
PC10MB         10mb unit for PC                                  1.00
PCBASE         PC base unit                                      1.00
PCCOLMON       PC colour monitor                                 1.00
PCKEY          PC keyboard                                       1.00

PC3            B&W 20MB Hard Disk PC             Location    Quantity
                                                 ----------  --------
PC20MB         20mb unit for PC                                  1.00
PCBASE         PC base unit                                      1.00
PCBWMON        Black and white monitor                           1.00
PCKEY          PC keyboard                                       1.00
```

Fig. 5.1.1.

for each component, its assembly level and the number of other stock items that use these components. The assembly level is set to zero if this component itself has no sub-assemblies. If it has one component then the assembly level is 1. A maximum of ten components are allowed for any assembly.

The link field is the number of other stock items that use that particular assembly. In other words a range of engines might use the same carburettor and the link field records the number of other engines, apart from the one whose stock details are being examined, that use that carburettor.

By pressing the Esc key you are returned to the main stock details screen. Esc again brings the SAGE request of **Post Abandon Delete**.

Thus all the details of a stock item and its components can be created and amended from the Update Stock Details screen.

5.2   Sales Order processing

The amount of detailed posting and reporting that has to be done when an order is received from a customer is considerable. Not all orders are straightforward. There may not be enough of a particular stock item immediately available to satisfy the order, or the credit of the customer may not be sufficient to cover the order. SAGE FINANCIAL CONTROLLER allows you to enter all the details of an order; it will then tell you if there are any exceptions, print the invoice and delivery note and update the ledgers. First of all you must select the Sales Order Processing option from the Main Menu. This will display a further menu:

> Enter Sales Orders
> Process Sales Order
> Enquiries
> Order Sheets
> Order Documents
> Despatch Notes
> Amend Dispatches

Update Ledgers
Delete Orders
Report Generator

Main Menu

When the first option is selected, Enter Sales Orders, a screen similar to the screen displayed when entering invoices directly. In the same way as the invoicing routine it divides the sequence into three parts; the heading, the details of the stock items required and the 'footing' detailing carriage, total price and notes to be printed on the invoice and delivery note. When you leave each sales order you are given the usual **Post Edit Abandon** options. The posting is actually done to a 'Back Order' file ready for the final processing which is normally performed whenever a batch of orders are received.

The second option is to process the Sales Orders and this will cause the allocation of stock to the orders whenever possible. This is very similar to the allocation of cash received against Sales Accounts. The allocation can be either Automatic or Manual. The allocations are made against every back order or outstanding order. An outstanding order would be one for which there was not sufficient stock initially available and so certain items have had to be held back until new stock has been received. Completed orders are ignored. The screen display will be similar to that shown in Fig. 5.2.1.

The Enquiries option allows you to display details of orders

Process Sales Order		Financial Controller			Date : 210386
Order No.	Date	Customer Name	Nett Amount	Allocate	Despatch
1	240186	Pegs Poodle Parlour	65.78	FULL	
2	240186	Hungry H Cafe	123.45	PART	
3	250186	HW Office Supplies	1000.25	FULL	
4	260186	GBH Garages	345.89	FULL	
5	260186	KW Hollis & Co.	90.34	NONE	

Method of Processing : Automatic Manual

Fig. 5.2.1.

PBTRB GOSLING

Order Sheets - Back Orders.

Date from : 010180
            to : 311299
          Page :   1

Order No.   :   1
Order Date : 050686

Customer Ref.   : AYGBO
Customer Name   : Aygro Foods Ltd.
Customer Address : 13 Green Street
                  : Alton on Sea
                  :
                  :

Customer Number   : 700012
Delivery Name   : ------ AS INVOICED ------
Delivery Address :
                  :
                  :
                  :

Notes   :
        :
        :

Taken By : Susan

Telephone Number : 01 010 21010

Delivery Date : 130686

Stock Code	Stock Description	Comment 1	Comment 2	Quantity	Dis't	Price
AC1	Sales Ledger Software			1.00	0.00	495.00
AC2	Purchase Ledger Software			1.00	0.00	495.00
AC3	Nominal Ledger Software			1.00	0.00	495.00
AC4	Invoicing Software			1.00	0.00	495.00

Carriage :   10.00   Order Total :   1980.00

```
Order No.   :    2              Customer Ref.    : BBLL            Customer Number : 12001
Order Date : 050686            Customer Name    : Bell Brothers Ltd   Delivery Name   : ------ AS INVOICED ------
                               Customer Address : 13, Brown Road,      Delivery Address :
Notes    :                                        Bradford,                            :
         :                                        W Yorks                              :
         :

Taken By : Ann                 Telephone Number : 0202 343432     Delivery Date   : 100686

Stock Code   Stock Description        Comment 1         Comment 2        Quantity Dis't   Price

PC1          B&W 10MB Hard Disk PC                                         1.00  5.00    2850.00
AC5          Integrated Accounts                                          1.00  0.00    1295.00
PT2          132 Column Printer                                           1.00  0.00     400.00
DK1          10 x 5.25" DS DD Disks                                       1.00  0.00      25.00
LP1          1 Part plain, box 2000 Sh                                    1.00  0.00      12.00
IS3          Plain Invoices 1000 Sheet                                    1.00  0.00      15.00
ST3          Plain Statements 2000 She                                    1.00  0.00      15.00
ST5          Payslips, box 1000 Sheets                                    1.00  0.00      15.00
                                                                         -----------
                                       Carriage :    25.00    Order Total :          4627.00
```

Fig. 5.2.2.

selected by order number, account reference and date range. The information given will supply the order number, data, name of the customer, the allocation and the despatch status. It means that customers can enquire regarding the status of their outstanding orders and discover if they have been completed and/or despatched. Further information on a second screen is available giving the details of what was ordered and when it was despatched.

An Order sheet will list details of any back orders,

```
***********************************
******      Peter Gosling    *******           ORDER ACKNOWLEDGEMENT
***********************************

Highfield House
Tower Road
Warfield
Worcs
WA4 6TR

Telephone  0123 45678

--------------------------------------------------------------------

Jason Industries Ltd                ACCOUNT REF.  JASON
Unit 12, Beech Ind Est
Freshwater                          ORDER NO.     10
Somerset
WL3 5TF                             DUE DATE      21/03/86

--------------------------------------------------------------------
```

Description	Unit	Quantity	Price	Value
Integrated Accounts	each	1.00	1295.00	1295.00
10 x 5.25" DS SD Disks	box	1.00	22.50	22.50

```
Total Order Value     1251.62
```

Fig. 5.2.3.

outstanding orders or despatched orders as shown in
Fig. 5.2.2. An outstanding order is one that has not been
despatched, but is ready for despatch.

The Order Document and Despatch Notes options will
produce the necessary pieces of paper defined in the text files

```
**************************************************      Highfield House
******      Peter Gosling      *******              Tower Road
**************************************************      Warfield, Worcs WA4 6TR
                                                   Telephone: 0123 45678


                                                   VAT No.: 123 4567 89

         Jason Industries Ltd                      Account Ref.      JASON
         Unit 12, Beech Ind Est
         Freshwater                                Invoice Date      12/10/87
         Somerset
         WL3 5TF                                   Invoice No.          7
```

QUANTITY	DETAILS	DISC	NETT PRICE	VAT
1.00	Integrated Accounts	5.00	1230.25	184.54
1.00	10 x 5.25" DS SD Disks	5.00	21.37	3.21

YOUR ORDER NO. : 78788

DELIVERY ADDRESS : ------ AS INVOICED ------

Total Nett	1251.62
Packing	0.00
VAT	187.75
TOTAL	1439.37

Fig. 5.2.4.

PETER GOSLING

Sales Order Proc. - Update Ledgers.

Date : 121087
Page : 1

Inv/Credit Number	Date	A/C	No.	N/C	Dep	Stock Code	Stock Description	Quantity	Nett Amount	Tc	Tax Amount
Invoice No.	7	121087	JASON	230	1210	7 AC5	Integrated Accounts	1.00	1230.25	T1	184.54
				231	1340	15 DK2	10 x 5.25" DS SD Di	1.00	21.37	T1	3.21

Fig. 5.2.5.

called SORDER.LYT and DESPATCH.LYT. These can be modified by means of the text editor available from the Utilities Menu. They are special report documents similar to INVOICE.LYT. A Sales Order acknowledgement form is shown in Fig. 5.2.3 and a Despatch Note in Fig. 5.2.4. With a Despatch Note only outstanding orders will be dealt with. The format of the despatch note and the invoice differ only in that the invoice document can be used for a credit note as well.

A Despatch Note can be amended before printing should you for some reason wish to amend the quantity of any stock item on the Note before despatch takes place. Be careful, however; you may only use this if the allocation has taken place but despatch has not.

Once all the Sales Order details have been completed as described above you may then update the Sales Ledger and Nominal Ledger. The same conditions apply as mentioned when an invoice is created regarding the Nominal Codes and Tax Codes. They can either be in the Stock Item section or the footing section, but not both. The details of postings are printed out as the posting takes place as shown in Fig. 5.2.5. You will be told if postings cannot take place because of the lack of necessary account information.

Orders that have been completed and despatched have no need to remain on the file once the ledgers have been updated. The Delete Orders option from the menu allows you to clear

```
| Process Purchase Orders  Financial Controller              Date : 121087 |

Order No.   Date          Supplier Name        Nett Amount  On-Order   Delivery
|      1    260987    M & T Office Supplies       126.78    ON-ORDER            |
|      2    260987    Amen Computers Ltd           99.80               COMPLETE |
|      3    270987    Highway Garage Ltd           45.67    ON-ORDER            |
|      4    270987    WB Oil Company              231.66    ON-ORDER            |
|      5    270987    M & T Office Supplies      1165.77                        |
```

Method of Processing : Automatic Manual

Fig. 5.3.1.

PETER GOSLING   Order Sheets - Outstanding Orders.

Date from : 010180
      to : 311299
    Page :   1

Order No.   :   5   Supplier Ref.   : SAGE   Supplier Number   :
Order Date : 050686   Supplier Name   : SAGESOFT PLC   Despatch Name   : ------ AS ORDERED ------
                               Supplier Address   : NEI House,   Despatch Address :
Notes :   : Regent Centre   :
      :   : Gosforth   :
      :   : Newcastle NE3 3DS   :

Placed By :   Telephone Number : 091 284 7077   Despatch Date :

Stock Code	Stock Description	Comment 1	Comment 2	Quantity	Dis't	Price
WP1	Word Processing Software			2.00	0.00	400.00
WP2	Spelling Checker			1.00	0.00	70.00
WP3	Mailmerge			1.00	0.00	70.00
			Carriage :	0.00	Order Total :	540.00

```
Order No.   :      6            Supplier Ref.        : ECHO                 Supplier Number   :
Order Date : 121087            Supplier Name        : Echo Electronics Ltd. Despatch Name     : ------ AS ORDERED ------
                               Supplier Address     : 19.Browning Mews,      Despatch Address  :
Notes       :                                         Halifax,                                 :
            :                                          W Yorks.                                 :
            :                                                                                   :

Placed By : Harry              Telephone Number : 0434 87654               Despatch Date : 211087

   Stock Code     Stock Description        Comment 1                Comment 2          Quantity Dis't  Price
   ----------  -----------------------  -----------------------  -----------------------  ---------------------------
   PC2         Colour 10MB Hard Disk PC                                                   3.00 10.00    8100.00
   PC2         Colour 10MB Hard Disk PC                                                   1.00 10.00    2700.00
   =========================================================================================================
                                                           Carriage :     0.00     Order Total :      10800.00
                                                                                                     ==========

Orders Total Value :    11340.00
```

Fig. 5.3.2.

PETER GOSLING

Order Sheets - Delivered Orders.

Date from : 010180
      to : 311299
    Page :   1

Order No.   :   1
Order Date : 050686

Supplier Ref.   : ABLE
Supplier Name   : Able Electronics Ltd.
Supplier Address : 13.Green Street,
                  : York
                  :
                  :

Supplier Number   :
Despatch Name   : ------ AS ORDERED ------
Despatch Address :
                  :
                  :

Notes :
       :
       :

Placed By :

Telephone Number : 0203 45678

Despatch Date : 100686

Stock Code	Stock Description	Comment 1	Comment 2	Quantity	Dis't	Price
PT1	80 Column Printer			2.00	0.00	440.00
PT2	132 Column Printer			2.00	0.00	640.00
PT3	220 Column Printer			2.00	0.00	1040.00

Carriage :   0.00   Order Total : 2120.00

```
Order No.  :      2              Supplier Ref.     : ECHO                 Supplier Number  :
Order Date : 050686             Supplier Name     : Echo Electronics Ltd. Despatch Name    : ------ AS ORDERED ------
                                Supplier Address  : 13,Browning Mews,      Despatch Address :
Notes  :                                          : Halifax,                                :
       :                                          : W Yorks.                                :
       :                                          :                                         :
       :

Placed By :                     Telephone Number : 0434 87654             Despatch Date    : 110686

Stock Code    Stock Description        Comment 1                 Comment 2                   Quantity Dis't  Price
-----------------------------------------------------------------------------------------------------------------
DK1           10 x 5.25" DS DD Disks                                                          10.00  0.00   120.00
DK3           10 x 5.25" SS DD Disks                                                          10.00  0.00   110.00
DK4           10 x 5.25" SS SD Disks                                                          10.00  0.00   100.00
DK8           10 x 3.25" DS DD Disks                                                          10.00  0.00   115.00
                                                                                             --------------------
                                                                 Carriage :     0.00     Order Total :        445.00
=================================================================================================================

Orders Total Value :    2665.00
```

Fig. 5.3.3.

from the files all those that are no longer to be processed.
Any partly completed orders will be ignored by this routine.
Should you attempt to delete an order that has either not been
posted or not been printed then SAGE will warn you. You
may only delete such a record if you really have a good
reason for wanting to.

```
#################################
######  Peter Gosling      #######            PURCHASE ORDER
#################################

  Highfield House
  Tower Road
  Warfield
  Worcs
  WA4 6TR

  Telephone   0123 45678

--------------------------------------------------------------------

  SUPPLIER                    ORDER NO.      6

  Echo Electronics Ltd.       ORDER DATE     12/10/87
  13,Browning Mews,
  Halifax,                    DELIVERY DATE  21/10/87
  W Yorks.
                              ORIGINATOR Harry

--------------------------------------------------------------------

  -----------------------------------------------------------------
  | Part Refernce |       Description       |Quantity|  Price |
  |---------------|-------------------------|--------|--------|
  |900/0002       |Colour 10MB Hard Disk PC |   3.00 | 3000.00|
  |900/0002       |Colour 10MB Hard Disk PC |   1.00 | 3000.00|
  |               |                         |        |        |
  -----------------------------------------------------------------


--------------------------------------------------------------------

  DELIVERY ADDRESS                 DELIVERY INSTRUCTIONS

  ------ AS ORDERED -------
```

Fig. 5.3.4.

5.3 Purchase Order processing

The processing of Purchase Orders follows exactly the same pattern as the processing of Sales Orders. Because a Purchase Order is not necessarily completed immediately the system will keep track of it until it is either completed or cancelled.

> Enter Purchase Orders
> Process Purchase Orders
> Enquiries
> Orders Sheets
> Order Document
> Amend Deliveries
> Delete Orders
> Report Generator
>
> Main Menu

Purchase Orders are entered in a manner similar to the entry of Sales Orders. When the Process Purchase Order option is chosen a screen as shown in Fig. 5.3.1 is displayed. It enables you to alter the status of each order and its delivery.

Enquiries will produce the same kind of information as when the Sales Order Processing option is in use. Orders sheets as shown in Fig. 5.3.2 and 5.3.3 are produced by the next option so that the current outstanding orders and delivered orders are detailed and an order document as shown in Fig. 5.3.4 is produced by the next option.

```
| Amend Deliveries            Financial Controller            Date : 270187 |

Order No.:  3                 Supplier Name:Highway Garage Ltd
A/C Ref. : HIGHW                  Notes  1 :
Date     : 260187                   "    2 :
Del Date : 310187                   "    3 :

Stock Code          Stock Description    Nett Amount   Quantity Ordered Delivered

DS1           10 x 5 1/4" DS DD disks      45.67        2.00    0.00      0.00




Quantity Delivered:
```

Fig. 5.3.5.

Once the order form has been created the next choice allows
you actually to set up the delivery by using the Amendment of
Deliveries through the sixth option producing a display as
shown in Fig. 5.3.5.

Orders can be deleted by the next choice.

The Purchase and Nominal Ledgers will not have postings
made to them via this routine. This has to be done at the time
of the receipt of the invoice from the supplier.

5.4   Multi-company use

FINANCIAL CONTROLLER enables you to keep the
accounts of a 'parent' and a number of 'subsidiary'
companies and must be used on a hard disk system. The
accounts of the separate subsidiary companies can be kept
separately but consolidated into the accounts of the parent.
The ledgers for the various subsidiary companies are set up
each in its own directory on the hard disk.

In order to set the system up for multi-company use you
have to set up a text file called COMPANY. This is set up
using SAGE text editor. COMPANY has to contain the
details of the directory where each set of files is located, the
name of each company and its address.

First of all create the directories for each subsidiary
company from the system prompt, C> if you are using a
hard disk. Do this by using the MS-DOS[2] command

C > md compa

for the creation of a directory called **compa** for the first
company. You could call the directories whatever you wish,
within reason, but it is a good idea to use names relating in
some way to the company names. To get into the directory
you need to use the MS-DOS command

C > cd \compa

The directory name is called a 'path' by SAGE and is enclosed
between backslash characters, \.

---

[2] MS-DOS is a trademark of Microsoft Corporation.

The COMPANY file is divided into sections separated by blank lines. Enter SAGE FINANCIAL CONTROLLER and from the Utilities sub menu go into the Text Editor. Create a file called COMPANY set out in the following pattern

```
PATH \parent\
PARENT
NAME 'Holding Company'
ADDRESS1 'World Buildings'
ADDRESS2 '35 Charity Street'
ADDRESS3 'Walford'
ADDRESS4 'Herts WL6 6TR'

PATH \holt\
SUBSIDIARY
NAME 'Holt Building Co. Ltd'
ADDRESS1 'Unit 5'
ADDRESS2 'Cowthorpe Industrial Estate'
ADDRESS3 'Walford'
ADDRESS4 'Herts WL4 8TZ'

PATH \radford\
SUBSIDIARY
NAME 'Radford Office Equipment'
ADDRESS1 'World Buildings'
ADDRESS2 '35 Charity Street'
ADDRESS3 'Walford'
ADDRESS4 'Herts WL6 6TR'
```

Each company can have its accounts dealt with separately and once the COMPANY file has been set up a menu of the company names is displayed for you to select the company for the next batch of postings.

Once the system is going you will need to consolidate the accounts into those of the parent company. This is done from the Utilities sub menu.

6 Utilities

On choosing the Utilities menu from the Main Menu you are presented with the following display.

> Initialisation
> Departments
> Reconfiguration
> Tax Code Changes
> DOS Functions
> Text Editor
>
> Main Menu

In the case of FINANCIAL CONTROLLER only there is a further option called 'Consolidation' enabling you to consolidate the accounts into those of the parent company as mentioned in the previous section.

The Initialisation option is used when you set up a SAGE accounting system. This is described in Chapter 1. The Departments option allows you to set up a number of departments, or cost centres, which can be used for analysis via the Report Generator.

Reconfiguration takes place at the end of every month, as was described in Chapter 2. Any changes in the VAT rates are taken care of by the next option. The DOS (Disk Operating System) functions that can be accessed through a SAGE system are

Print: to print a document or file stored on disk. This would be used if you had decided not to print a report immediately it is generated but to save the printing until later.

Copy: to make a copy of a file on another disk.

Rename: To change the name of any file.

Delete: to delete a file from disk.

Directory: the equivalent of the DOS DIR command.

Edit: takes you directly into the Text Editor so that you can edit or create documents.

The Text Editor is a simple wordprocessing package allowing you to create documents; reports, invoices, order forms and debt-chasing letters.

In addition to these utilities SAGE offers you two more which are accessed from outside the system. These are located on the program disk and are called UTIL3 and UTIL9. In order to use them you have to leave SAGE and return to your A or C prompt. By typing the utility name — UTIL3 or UTIL9 — they will be set into action.

Both these programs, when run, display a warning that you should telephone SAGE before using them to make sure that you will be doing no damage to the system when the program is working (*see* Fig. 6.1).

UTIL3 is a program that allows you to amend certain items on the ledgers.

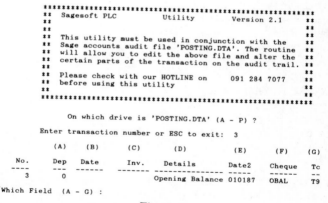

Fig. 6.1.

```
**************************************************************
**   Sagesoft PLC           Utility9        Version 1.00    **
**                                                          **
**                                                          **
**   This utility must be used in conjunction with the      **
**   Sage Accountant Range.  Its purpose is to reset the    **
**   Turnover figure for all Sales and Purchase Accounts    **
**   to zero (0.0)                                          **
**                                                          **
**   Please check with our HOTLINE on      091 284 7077     **
**   before using this utility                              **
**                                                          **
**************************************************************

          On which drive are the Accounts files (A - P) ?
```

Fig. 6.2.

Having selected the field to be changed you can enter the
amended entry.

UTIL9 is a program that zeros the turnovers of every
account.

When you have entered the drive letter the zeroing takes place
immediately and the name of each account is flashed up as it
is processed.